THE ROAD BEFORE US

THE ROAD
BEFORE
US

100
GAY BLACK POETS

ASSOTO SAINT

1991   GALIENS PRESS   NEW YORK, NY

This is a trade paperback original from Galiens Press,
Box 4026, 524 West 23rd Street,
New York, NY 10011

First edition, first printing: October 1991

Library of Congress Cataloging-in-Publication Data

The Road before us : 100 gay Black poets / edited by Assoto Saint. —
    1st ed.
        p. cm.
    ISBN 0-9621675-1-7 : $10.00
    1. Gay men—Poetry. 2. Gays' writings, American. 3. Afro-
American gays—Poetry. 4. American poetry—Afro-American authors. 5.
American poetry—20th century. I. Saint, Assoto, 1957-
PS595.H65R6 1991
811'.54080353—dc20   91-30117
                                                        CIP

In loving memory
of
Redvers JeanMarie
David Warren Frechette
Ortez Alderson

Depending on how you see the times
we're wasting time or in a moving line

Deee-Lite

TABLE OF CONTENTS

X

xii

xiii

XV

PREFACE

The Road Before Us could have taken a far different path. As its editor and co-publisher, what I wanted foremost was a collection that would provide one more stepping-stone on the road to gay black poetical empowerment. Too often this has been the road not taken.

Each poet in this volume is represented by one poem. Many faces, facets, and phases of our lives are painted in these selections. From the ancient African tribal shamanistic tradition, as in Craig A. Reynolds "The moon singers," to the common contemporary father/son alienation, as in "Bermuda" by Jim Murell — we explore, we examine, we experience.

Some poems, such as Thomas Glave's glorious "Landscape in black" and Arthur Wilson's gut-wrenching, lay-it-all-out "One rawdog night when too much of my queer was showing," are epic in stature. Others, such as Rickey Butler's poignant "After the fuck" and Richard Witherspoon's delicious "Haiku," offer the precise minimum of words and images needed to make their effect.

Carl Cook's tender "Love letter #25" and Bil Wright's evocative "Miracle" are sensual paeans to defiant sex and love in the era of AIDS. Blackberri's sweet "Love song" and André De Shields' wicked "His(blues)story" are lyrics. Three contributions are short prose pieces that read well poetically.

I relish this mixture of styles, which are as wide-ranging as our concerns. The myths, metaphors, and mundaneness of our gay black community, like those of any other community, broaden and deepen everyone's knowledge of what it is to be human.

Among the poets included, Melvin Dixon and Essex Hemphill's writings are of paramount importance. The images they weave with their pens are extraordinary and would stand out in any company at any time. It is almost impossible for any openly gay poet to get his work published, and a number of the poets here, have followed Hemphill's example and put out their own collections. However, most of the poets in this anthology have never appeared in a book before.

Check out Robert Westley's brutally honest "What's happening." Read aloud Marvin K. White's fiercely humorous "Last rights." How about Metaphora's glorious homage to the gender-bending vogue culture in "Poem for the club kids?" It is my dream that all these fine young writers will keep penning poetry, polishing their craft, and juicing up a literally dying art.

*   *   *

The title *The Road Before Us* is borrowed from a line in the poem "Hejira" that the late Redvers JeanMarie wrote about our friendship. He dedicated it to me. I cherish it. It is anthologized here. The choice of "gay black poets" rather than "black gay poets" was a personal one. I originally used the working subtitle *Gay African-American Poets* — to which some contributors strongly objected because they were not born in the United States and moreover have not chosen to naturalize as American citizens, as I have.

Afrocentrists in our community have chosen the term "black gay" to identify themselves. As they insist, black comes first. Interracialists in our community have chosen the term "gay black" to identify themselves. As they insist, gay comes first. Both groups' self-descriptions are ironically erroneous. It's not which word comes first that matters, but rather the grammatical context in which those words are used — either as an adjective or as a noun. An adjective is a modifier of a noun. The former is dependent upon the latter.

I have never labeled myself either Afrocentrist or interracialist. From reading or seeing my theater pieces, many might characterize me as an Afrocentrist; but others might immediately characterize me as an interracialist because I have loved and lived with a white man for the past eleven years.

Although I make no excuses or apologies for the racially bold statements in my writings, I also owe no one any justification of my "till-death-do-us-part" interracial relationship. While the *black gay* vs. *gay black* debate rages on, in much-needed constructive dialogue, we'd best ponder, as L. Lloyd Jordan did at the conclusion of his essay "Black Gay vs. Gay Black" (*BLK*, June 1990), "Who are gay blacks and black gays? Halves of a whole. Brothers."

Furthermore I consider my sexuality a preference. Most of us have an inclination to bisexuality that we don't acknowledge or act upon. I am very proud of my gayness, which is not to be confused with homosexuality.

In the preface to his book *Gay Spirit*, Mark Thompson explains this distinction clearly: "Gay implies a social identity and consciousness actively chosen, while homosexual refers to a specific form of sexuality. A person may be homosexual, but that does not necessarily imply that he or she would be gay." I declare that a person may be gay, but not necessarily homosexual.

Color (and it is so much more than skin pigmentation) is not a preference. The same has not to this day been scientifically demonstrated regarding our gayness, which is so much more than sexual orientation. It's hard to imagine that any writer in this anthology would ever want to change either his color or his gayness, given a choice.

I realize that these views add fuel to the "fire and brimstone" pronouncements of those in far-right politics who argue that we lesbians and gays could change to "normal" if we wanted to.

While I agree with our lesbian and gay community's tenet that some of us can't change, I would stand up anytime to Jesse Helms and his ilk, and declare loudly that, whatever the case may be, *I refuse* to change. Far too many of us continuously let church and state dictate our fate, by submitting to their painful spiritual and political butt-fuck.

What does all this politics have to do with poetry? As Judy Grahn said in a keynote address at OutWrite '90, "Poetry predicts us, tells us where we are going next."

Shouldn't we, the poets in this anthology, dispatch to Helms our gay black poems each time he gets up in front of the Senate and spews forth yet another homophobic or racist harangue without fairness of debate and real challenge? Couldn't fifty of us (one representing each state of siege that he wants to turn our USA into) also fax him full-size etchings of our dicks to be inserted in *The Congressional Record*. Then ours would not be the dicks of death as popularly characterized, but truly the dicks of everlasting political life.

* * *

Some months ago, I urged all the contributors who are HIV-positive or have AIDS to come out. I felt then, and I still feel, that there is nothing that those of us in this predicament could reveal in our bios that is more urgent and deserving of mention than our seropositivity or diagnosis.

A number of contributors agreed. I applaud their trust and thrust. Others who have previously come out publicly chose not to do so in this instance. A few whom I know to be in the last stages of HIV illness cited confidentiality, and their right of privacy.

While sympathetic to the right of privacy issue, I also find it part of the overall problem. It fosters anonymity rather than visibility. And when we don't show en masse the lives, the faces, and the hearts of AIDS — ours included — we are accepting all the connotations of shame, all the mystification of sin and repentance that those who are plainly simple-minded place on a virus.

AIDS is a Pandora's box. There is real jeopardy in revealing seropositivity, publicly or privately. In gay black poetry, the issue has been primarily dealt with from a third-person narrative rather than a first-person focus.

Meanwhile, in highly disproportionate numbers compared to our percentage in the American population, and adding to the lowering of our expected paltry sixty-year-or-so life span as black men, there are many gay disappearing acts among us, too often played solo, or for a small — and not so captive — audience. As the late Joseph Beam, editor of *In the Life*, anticipated and stated: "These days the nights are cold-blooded and the silence echoes with complicity."

So far no one has given me a valid explanation for Beam's silence regarding his illness. (For those who may not know, his body was discovered in an advanced stage of decomposition.) What kind of indictment of his preaching on behalf of the gay black community is that, for him not to have reached out to us? What kind of indictment is that of us, especially those who were privy to his AIDS diagnosis, for not having fully reached out to him?

Back in April 1988, Joe stayed overnight at my apartment as he always did when he visited New York City. I detected the syndrome beneath the moodiness, innuendoes, and fungus of the fingers. I did not disclose to him my own seropositivity, although thinking of it now, I believe that he detected more than just holocaust obsession in the poems I shared with him.

What kind of "deadly guessing" game were Joe and I, two of the better-known gay black writers, supposedly leaders, and most importantly friends, playing with each other? What kind of label do I attach to my name, after leaving unreturned messages on his answering machine, for not marching down to Philadelphia and knocking on/down his door?

Yes, I am sick of the destructive threats that HIV constantly poses to my life-partner, my lovers, my friends, my communities, and me. On my desk, pictures of Redvers, David, and Ortez, to whose memory this anthology is dedicated, are framed like icons.

Each time I write, I hear their voices, backed by a chorus of others I loved ("One AIDS death every eight minutes; it ain't enough to write; you gotta demonstrate") pound in my head, like those sanctifying drums, especially *tambou assôto*, I used to hear, in my childhood, in Haiti, in the hours of darkness.

* * *

May the rhythm of our gay black hearts be as uplifting in our daily lives as it is in our essays, anthologies, films, rallies, one-night-stands, and poems.

May the rhetoric never rage like the grandstand of many pedantics in the gay white community, which we so often hasten to castigate for claiming to speak on behalf of our "rainbow" community.

And most of all, may we come to believe in each other — heroes, first, to ourselves — unafraid to "strike a pose" and take a stand.

Ours is a country where omens abound out of control. Ours is a country tempted by fascism. Ours is a country in a demythologized age, perhaps void of salvation. Yet I don't believe in the destruction of America, but in a reconstitution that recognizes our fully participating gay black voices. Silence = Death. Writing = Life. Publishing = Survival.

With sixty T-cells left, I live on borrowed time. However, self-pity and sympathy are not part of my survival kit — another factor why making this book a reality became a first priority.

But when I do die, killed like hundreds of thousands in this AIDS war, may it transpire that every Memorial Day — until the circus of media, clown masks of stigma, and jeers of hysteria stop in our country; and certainly until a cure is found, or at least until a do-or-die governmental, scientific, and societal commitment to discover one finally gets underway — my life-partner, mother, lovers, friends, fellow poets, somebody, anybody... burn the Stars and Stripes, then toss the ashes over my grave.

And please don't sing "The Star-Spangled Banner" — but, furiously, read back every poem in the following pages.

Assoto Saint, *nom de guerre*
Summer 1991
New York City

ACKNOWLEDGMENTS

I wish to thank all the contributors to this anthology for sharing their work and making this volume possible. I am particularly grateful to the following contributors: Oye Apeji Ajanaku; Akhenaton for his unconditional friendship, humor, and sharp eyes while he assisted me with editing; Thom Bean; Blackberri; Rodney Dildy; Melvin Dixon; Sean Drakes; the late David Frechette who even on his hospital deathbed helped me to resolve certain problems with the manuscript; Thomas Glave for his editorial assistance; Kenton Grey for his incredible patience in typesetting the book; Mark Haile; Craig G. Harris for his editorial assistance; Essex Hemphill; Isaac Jackson; the late Redvers JeanMarie who left me a legacy which I used as seed money for this project; Joseph Long; Jamez Smith; Vega; Marvin White; Arthur T. Wilson and Bil Wright.

In addition, I wish to thank the following individuals and organizations for their encouragement and assistance: Franklin Abbott; Leif Ahlgren; Mark Ameen; Maceo Anderson and his life-partner Dennis Rager; Willie C. Barnes; the late Rotimi Fani-Kayode for his photograph on the back cover; Michael Lassell; Michael Lee; Jim Marks; Al Meynet; Pedro Perez for his design of the cover; the late Bradley S. Phillips; Don Reid for his painting on the front cover; Marlon Riggs; Sapphire; Bree Scott-Hartland; Charles Michael Smith for a superb proofreading of the galleys; David Trinidad; Phil Wilkie; Aaron Woodruff; Gay Men of African Descent; Men of All Colors Together; Other

Countries; The Black Gay and Lesbian Leadership Forum; the New York State Council on the Arts for awarding me a poetry fellowship, and my co-workers at the Health and Hospitals Corporation in New York City.

I am especially appreciative of the constant support of my therapist Michael Shernoff; my cousin Rachel Cassion Alerte; and my mother Marie Lubin. Carl Morse contributed valuable advice, and also a superb proofreading of the galleys. I am indebted to publicist Michele Karlsberg for her indefatigable promotion of the book.

Finally, I want to acknowledge my life-partner Jaan Urban Holmgren who blessed me with peace, love and much strength while urging me on *The Road Before Us*.

THE ROAD BEFORE US

LAWRENCE DEWYATT ABRAMS, III

UNFULFILLED MIRACLES

I.

He was cute the first night
he threw his legs to Jesus
in the backseat
of a dark-blue Honda Accord
with Jersey plates.

The boys on the pier
didn't have to listen for screams.
They knew the white guy
with pasty hands
    red cheeks
    big dick
    brass knuckles
    and bad politics.
He always paid for his passion
in crisp fifties and tipped well
if you bled and called him daddy
between your screams.

II.

He was still cute the second night
he threw his legs to Jesus
in the backseat
of a dull-green Chevy
that smelled of stale beer
and incense.

1

This trick didn't seem to mind
his slight odor.
The man even asked about the scars
as he rode the boy's bent back.
Words stifled on his lips.
The trick was only paying for flesh,
not answers —
business was business.

The dark-skinned man with the accent
who drove the dull-green Chevy
promised to return next payday.

He paid in small bills
and left no signs of his cumming
or his passing.

III.

He was still cute on the third night
he threw his legs to Jesus
in the penthouse apartment
where somebody was having a party.

He never knew
what was in the drink they gave him
but it covered well for the syringe
that came after.

2

He thought he heard
someone say he was a doctor
but he didn't leave a calling card.

He remembered
    the camera
    bright lights
    two other young bodies
    the hands
    and voices laughing:
        "It's my turn!"
        "It's my turn!"
        "It's my turn!"

They took him without paying.

IV.

On the fourth night it rained
and no one got to see how cute he was.

V.

He was still cute on the fifth night
he threw his legs to Jesus
in a one-room dump on the Deuce.

He got twice the going rate
'cause the trick left
the glove at home.

3

He even got to shower
before the manager came
to change soiled sheets.

As the water ran over him
he was having trouble
remembering   names.

VI.

He was tired on the sixth night
he stumbled into Jesus' arms.

He sat silently in the church
and opened his heart and tried to pray.

And he couldn't
remember the words.

VII.

He was still cute on the seventh morning
lying in the arms of Jesus.

The priest told the police
he heard the second gunshot
but not the first.

4

OYE APEJI AJANAKU

THE WIND AND THE OCEAN
(ON MY HOMOSEXUALITY III)

From what cause comes the howling wind?
What phantom warning sets it in raging motion?
Is it prophecy of an imminent fate descending,
        approaching,
Or caution of lurking dangers,
Our constant companion,
Our nautical kin?

The wind,
Peeling spray from the climaxed crest
        of great angry swells,
Whips a cold wetness up
From the bow's sharp cutting keel
And lays it on the afterbow;
On me,
Standing alone here, battered by the gales,
Salt-soaked and awe-inspired,
In sacred communion with the raw elements
        and forces,
Those yet to be calmed or claimed
        by men.

As I listen to the omen in the wind,
I scan the great infinity before me:
The vast expanse of a stormy ocean,
Always stretching, unending,
        forever in motion!
The constant surge, the swell,
The wild, the tumultuous,
The unrelenting!
The roll, the roll, and the sway...

5

And I know that my inner movings are patterned,
Like my need for the touch and the love
           of other men—
Are forever patterned after these.
And the power that moves through me,
Through my nature and my being,
Is the same as the forces of the ocean
           and the wind.

Let the salt spray sting on my face,
And I communicate with an ocean!
And I am enraptured!

O to ride the tempest and weather the storm,
And feel the ocean around you as you listen to the wind!

Listen to the wind.

At sea, circa 1963

6

AKHENATON

COOL WAVES

Jasmine-scented winds
Cool waves waft into this room
Blacker than the night
Here we lie having spent all
Our creative energies

SABAH AS-SABAH

INVOCATION

I want to fuck a skinhead
hard
ripping flesh
thrust all twelve inches of black
down his sewered hole
I want a Bible placed under
his sweat-drenched face
my nails digging into his bald head
slamming both spit and blood
on the Holy Scriptures

READ IT
"And God said..."
READ IT
"And Ham saw his father's nakedness..."
READ IT
*"And Ham saw his father's nakedness
and cursed his sons to be servants of servants..."*

I want to whip you with my dick
drawing up welts on your pale
ass
sweat-poppin'
smellin' of sour milk, fatback and hoppin' johns
I'm gonna pump history darker
with every stroke
Take it all
All four hundred years of semen
piled hot to explode
as a cross on your pained face

CALL MY NAME
"Nigger"
CALL MY NAME
"Jigaboo"
CALL MY NAME
"Colored"
CALL MY NAME
"Black"
CALL MY NAME
"African"

I want to fuck a skinhead
so deep
that his soul aches
that his mama's soul aches
and his grandmother's soul moans
So deep that his ancestors vomit my scum
affronting heaven
Hail to the Father
Hail to the Son
Hail to the Holy Ghost
Feel my baptism, bastard
Feel my baptism

THOM BEAN

A LOVE POEM FOR WHITE BOYS
WHO DON'T KNOW WHO I AM

hey baby
is this what integration is all about
these white smiles
these sweet caresses
you're giving out in public
are not for me

i am a black gay male
i live my life alone
invisible to most of you
a non-entity ignored
shunned
even after sex
especially after sex

i am your gorilla fantasy
i suffer your tiresome presumptions
i give myself too freely
i am too solicitous

i am the trick you turn to
and never really love
i am desired at night
and never treated the same
in daylight

after all
what would people think
your friends might not understand
your peccadillo
your aberration

i am entertainment tonight
as convenient and disposable
as kleenex

i am the living dildo on which
you seek your comic and tragic relief
i am the chair upon which
you sit your frustrations
and base your superiority

i am just a nigger to you
even though my credentials
are of the highest order

you do not understand
(or care)
when i tell you
i am exploited
taken for granted
seldom given what is due me

my gifts are never returned
by you
my anguish is never heard
by you
who i am is not important
to you

an endangered species
my beauty and spirit denied
i am the "no blacks" referred to

in classifieds

i am the foot you step on
in your bar
without ever looking back
i am the one you mock
to make yourself feel better

still a stranger in my own community
not a member of your tribe
i am a nomad
patronized and rejected
at every turn

seldom hired
often fired
never promoted
when acknowledged
i sometimes forget who i am
but you are always there
to remind me in countless ways
just like a pimp

i am your whore
you fuck with my existence
yet you wonder why
i am angry

until it is too late
until i go off
until i rob you

until i kill you
or until i die
even then you may not notice
who i am
justice for me is elusive
always in the future

you own where i live
what i buy
where i go
you've stolen my art
my dreams
my music
do you want to trivialize my soul too

it hurts me that my blackness
is still enslaved
(privacy for a slave is inexcusable)
but you are not my master
my god anymore
i am not a game
for your amusement

i don't need you
to define me
to explain away my mystery
i already know who i am
if you really want to know me
bring all your stuff with you
not just lust or need

to accept me
is a political statement
about who we really are
to deny me is to deny yourself

you think i am too militant
when i get this way
you want to critique
theorize
do a paper or a thesis
on how i should speak
feel
act
think
dress
because i won't allow you
to disrespect me anymore
because finally
i am taking back my power

if you can ascend
to the top of the whitest strata
and rationalize me out of existence
remember what i told you
you will always be
just another faggot like me
by the same reasoning process
that reduces me to being
just another nigger

once you and i get over that phobia

break with tradition
become free to set new values
establish our own social icons
you will see
that color is just another
inconsequential barrier
to cross

i could be your lover
unless you are too white for me
i could be your friend
unless i am too black for you
we could be allies
unless we are too afraid
to find ourselves
in each other

BLACKBERRI

LOVE SONG

1.
you move me to poetry
to song
you're often in my thoughts
are my thoughts
moving me to poetry
to song
then to poetry

2.
even your silence
tells me things
your heart can't
and when you are near
you can no more
maintain than i

3.
in a dream
i loved you long
and deep
you let go
i let go
without a touch
i awoke wet
surprised

4.
you move me to poetry
to song
you're in my fantasies
are my fantasies
realized
realize
you are moving me to poetry
to song
then to poetry
again

ERIC STEPHEN BOOTH

AN EXERCISE IN MISOGYNY

So I lied and told her that I loved her
Starved, she took me seriously
My heart couldn't make a U-turn
Out of pity I married her

I hit her when I was wrong, then gave her
Roses with thorns to reconfirm our vows
Out of fear of being exposed
Growing up just like dad

Through journeys of weekend violence
It dawned on me after our fourth child
That my heart wasn't steering
And my brain was on automatic drive

She damned me to hell
My mother couldn't believe her ears
After a lifetime of masculine strife
I came face to face with my fears

BERNARD BRANNER

T'AIN'T NOBODY'S BIZNESS

there ain't nothing
i can do
or nothing i can say
that folks don't criticize me
but i'm gonna do
what i want to
anyway
and i don't care
what people say. *

a' course
they wondered more
than once
why the pouting lips
betrayed the melancholy
eyes/
why the bloody nails
attached to dainty wrists
moved so rigorously
through spiked and glossy
hair/or smoothed
the pants too tight
to testify
before any judge
and jury

slut/whore
daughter of a whore
always just a tad
too loud at parties
the laugh too long
to accommodate the joke
she drank much too much
to partake of holy sacrament

and upon parting
her friendly peck
begot a trail
a' spit

brazen hussy/sister
girl-friend-a-mine
i asked one day
why the walk so super
sensual
the talk so slick
and breathy
"...incest survivor"
she said
"incest survivor"

*i swear i won't call
no coppa
if i'm beat up
by my papa
t'ain't nobody's bizness
if i do.* *

* "T'ain't Nobody's Bizness If I Do" by P. Grainger and E. Robbins
MCA Music (ASCAP).

RORY BUCHANAN

BARBECUES

I was taught
men marry women
have two point five kids
ranch homes in suburbs
with impossibly green lawns
surrounded by
pristine white picket fences
shop at pathmark and k-mart
buy tools from sears
go to church every sunday
pray for salvation
find mistresses when bored

I was told
it was wrong to
love another man
touch the way I do
mingle spirits and fluids
feel okay about who I am
listen to my heart
expose the real me
admit to being gay

I was warned
that if I followed my
unconventional desires
slept with a man
satisfied wants
fulfilled needs
I would burn in hell
fry forever

So
I tell them
"Start the barbecue"

JOHN E. BUSH

REMEMBER ME

Remember me for the love I gave
and tried to give
for the companionship we shared
held dear
remember me.

Although I would have liked
our time together to have been longer
so much I wanted to do
so much you expected of me
it was not to be
still remember me.

Think about those good times
when we laughed and dined
at the table of fellowship
good times now gone
yet preserved forever in your memory
remember me.

Know that my love for you
was not one that was duty-bound
but it emerged sincerely
from some unknown place
a love once mine
now left to you to hold
and pass on to others
when it is your turn to leave
so remember me.

Not in a sorrow of despair
but triumphantly
remember me.

CHUCK BUTLER

BOURGEOIS AT TWENTY

He chose 2 wear blue
shorts real short
with the hamstring muscles exposed
4 all 2 see
how magnificent
athletics
good genes and
sculpture can be

Black shiny good hair
was unassuming
under a maroon baseball cap
that said "Temple" and "Hello
I am gorgeous"
a mandatory leather gym bag
sat on the seat
next 2 him

He shelled and popped
pistachio nuts
in his mouth while reading *Newsweek*
or some cousin
and oh yes
his bulge lay cocked
like a .38
pointing west

RICKEY BUTLER

AFTER THE FUCK

when the sheets are up
the curtains drawn
and your eyes get all fuzzy
because of the sun
don't disappear

BLAND J. "BJ" CARR

ODE TO JAMES BALDWIN

The writer/man knows how
to move me.
His pen drips
liquid, elegant prose.
He knows
how
to caress a mind.
Listen well:
He turns a tight phrase.
His metaphors are
yesterday/today/tomorrow's
street talk.
His words are
grandad's down-home blues/
grandma's church songs/
Rev.'s rhythmic gospel idiom.
Listen well.

DON CHARLES

PONY BOY

White man
Wealthy man
Bed is cold
Body old
Black man
Healthy man
Firm and young
Heavy hung

Silver man
Pays to score
Horny guy
Out to buy
Mocha man
Plays the whore
Life is hell
Got to sell

Business man
Undercover
Hotel suite
So discreet
Hustler man
Hired lover
Money's right
Spends the night

Respected man
Life of leisure
Owns the town
Sneaks around
Survivor man
Selling pleasure
Rich man's toy
Pony boy

J. COLEMAN

WHEN I WRITE TO GODMOTHER

I'm careful with   Language
Slang takes a holiday

careful not to twist   my tongue
She must not hear the   loose metaphor nights

nor smell the necks I've licked —

I don't smack my lips
She must not see   the boys I've kissed
nor hear the whispers —

She must not examine my prose   for nuance
nor read between
too many lines —

But if asked
I won't deny perdition —
What price   a letter!

I feel pen pricks
in my soul.

With a clean sheet of paper in hand
and newly brushed teeth   I ask

"How are you?"

CARL COOK

LOVE LETTER #25

September has
the clearest air
the coolest nights
the brightest moons lie still
like autumn leaves
I am renewed
by thoughts of you

Tomorrow
my love
I may need to wear a raincoat
galoshes made of manufactured latex
an umbrella wide enough
to keep us dry
in a sudden storm

But I am
of the faith
that storms will pass
the rains will dry
and love as cool and clear
as September air
will still be ours

ANDRE DE SHIELDS

HIS(BLUES)STORY

Verse I

Before there was Desdemona,
Iago would warm Othello's bed.
Before there was Desdemona,
Iago would warm Othello's bed.
He would sharpen his sword,
Fill his lamp with oil,
And rub his woolly head.

Verse II

Before Caesar knew Cleopatra,
He would hold Mark Antony to his chest.
Before Caesar knew Cleopatra,
He would hold Mark Antony to his chest.
And that's why the Queen of the Nile
Invited a serpent to make a home in her breast.

Stop Time

Now Achilles destroyed the Trojans
Because of a boy in his tent.
And if it hadn't been for Jimmy Baldwin,
Young Giovanni would've had no rent.
When Alexander marched out of Egypt,
He was fierce; he was festive; he was grand.
And when Jesus chose his disciples,
He made everyone a man.

30

So, when you study your history,
You'd better learn it like you should.
    'Cause after God created the Heavens and the Earth,
    And separated the light from the darkness,
    And divided the water from the waters,
    And gathered the dry land from the seas,
    And produced vegetation according to its kind,
    And hung the moon, and sun, and stars in the sky,
    And threw birds in the air and fish in the ocean,
    And placed wild creatures in the forest,
    God said: "I'm lonely. I think I'll make Me a man
    In My image."
    And, so, He did.
    Then, God looked around at all He had done and shouted:
"This is good."

RODNEY G. DILDY

HEROES

The heroes have died
Died twisting to blind
leadened boogies
Died broken blue midst indigo
moods, sworded bone
unsheathed ivory
blood-burned biceps
Died cold-dredged
worm-swollen
thru mute catfish alleys
My heroes
they have all died
over or underqualified
neglected or exposed
from genius and gross
stupidities
Died dirty-nailed
greasy-necked
Died gem-cysted
diamond-eyed

MELVIN DIXON

LAND'S END

Zero ground, fickle sandbar
where graves and gravity conspire,

Beer bottle amber and liquor green
surrender their killing shards.

Like ashes, dust, even glass
turns back into what it was.

Skeletal driftwood and seaweed hair
beg for a body. Any body.

Yet all you see is surf out there,
simply more and more of nothing.

If you must leave us, now or later,
the sea will bring you back.

Provincetown

SEAN DRAKES

LOVE LESSON #1

To Richard Cousar, whose death to AIDS encourages safer-sex
behavior, drives knowledge-sharing, stimulates my artistic responses
to the epidemic and has taught me what love feels like.

I.
A summer Sunday on Christopher Street
brought us together:
Two black gay men
yearning for love.
Quicker than instantly,
we shared secrets, passion,
weekends and underwear.
Suddenly, my six months exhausted,
I had to package
then file
this ideal come true.
I was twenty-one,
he, forty-three,
and rekindling
a thirteen-year romance
as I coped with foreign feelings.

II.
The bright winter moon
guided me —
a messenger of goodwill
and faith
in a plastic pouch —
to and from his hospital
bedside.
Day by day,
kisses,
hugs
and offerings failed
to salvage my friend,
till after I hung up the phone,
a restless night
became
endless.

ERROL A. EDWARDS

GOING DOWN

Emotions fell overboard as
Your eager tongue washed my body.
Waves of ecstasy pounded and
I drowned in your caress.

TROYNELL EDWARDS

FUCK ME

FUCK ME HOW FAGGOTS LIKE IT
FUCK ME HOW PROSTITUTES LIVE IT/
HARD AND QUICK FUCK ME
ON MY HEAD/ON FLOORS/IN HALLWAYS
FUCK ME STRAIGHT
FUCK ME LIKE YOU'D FUCK YOUR WIFE
— WITH RESPECT

ABBA ELETHEA

EARTHBOUND HEAVENSOUND

For Leonard

We make music:
sticks staccato strike
plastic bucket bottom
stuck between sneakers
stomping a steady grin
of amplified air space;
Snapped against concrete
a bass drum back-beat
of Broadway bop

The Blackyouth's body
arrhythmic blur
His mid-town center-stage:
The corner, the curb —
Broadway & 45th
He riffs:
Boodidly didly didly didly
Chu gong gong gong gong
Dotalaa dotalaa dotalaa dotalaa
Deedaduh deedaduh deedaduh
Deedala deeddala deedala
Dah dah dah boom
Chu gong chu gong
Chu gong gong gong gong
Bo Diddly didly didly
Bop bop bop

A child:
beneath his teens —
Sings his dreams?
Drums his whole song

culling crowds to circle
clamor clap & cling
Shoulder to shoulder
smiling they ring
this budding *Max Roach*
of bucket bop —
beneath his teens
drumming his dreams!

In greasy tee-shirt
unwashed jeans;
He screams
a rapid fire
pistol crackin'
polyrhythmic
jungle trackin'
ass hawlin'
ancestor callin'
loud insistent
swinging sound —
MID-TOWN:
Amid the busy blare
of night
its garish light
on the curb
on the corner
on Broadway
We make music.

We make music
from a turned-down

washtub
stick and string
Standing in the
Ferry Terminal
thumping up
pocket change
In a range
of true stringed
bass viole
Capped in *King Cole*
lyric timbre
Shu boom boom boom doo baa
Doo baa doo oooouuuu doo baa
Ooouuu bee dooo baa doo baa
Doo baa baa dee
Boo baa deeda boo doo baa
Doo baa baa dee
Shu boom boom boom boo daa
Doo baa doo ooouuu doo baa
Deedaa deedaa deedaa
Deeboom boom
Dee daa daa dee

We make music
inside a crazed hell
raised in GNP's... IT's
LBO's and JB's
We make music
We make music
To wring a smile
from an evil child
WE MAKE MUSIC!

40

LARRY FERGUSON

SHADE

eyes cold & desolate
like some lunar landscape
you see victim
I want passion
thinking you will fuck
my brains out
but you want to bash them
with your fist
in revenge
for some man
who first clutched your piece
at age nine
you learned what a prize
you possess
between your legs
that erection
more reflex than desire
Air Jordans ain't cheap

SALIH MICHAEL FISHER

WHOREGRAPHICS

BLACK GAY MEN ARE WHORES
THEY ARE ARTISTS CHANGING FACES
WITH THEIR CREATIVE GENIUS
WHORES WHO CAN HIDE BEHIND CLOWN MASKS
OF STRAIGHTNESS FOR SURVIVAL AND DAY-TO-DAY LIVING
WHORES WHO GIVE YOU BUTCH AND QUEEN IN ONE SENTENCE
THEN FAST SEVERE CONTORTED LOOKS IN ANOTHER
THEY ARE ARTISTS PAINTING THAT CANVAS CALLED AMERICA
AND YOU WOULD NEVER KNOW YOU'VE BEEN READ LIKE A BOOK

WHORES HAVE NO SHAME ABOUT WHAT THEY ARE
DON'T MIND STEPPING IN CARS OF TRUTH
KNOWING THAT THE DOORS OF NASTY HYPOCRISY
SOMETIMES WILL CATCH THEIR FINGERS AND HURT THEM
WE BLEED YES AIN'T NOTHING NEW
WE KNOW WHO WE ARE BUT WE BE TRUE
WE LOVE OURSELVES BECAUSE NO ONE ELSE WILL
WE UNDERSTAND OUR CREATIONS AND THE ART OF GAYNESS
LOVING AND HURTING BROTHERS WHO ARE OUR BEST FRIENDS

GUY-MARK FOSTER

PASSIVE RESISTANCE

time and again
on a cold floor
he says the same things
i squirm free
my rabbit-butt perched
high in the air
promises nothing
he cannot find
elsewhere
yet i wiggle it
beneath his nose
aware the scent
reels him
in

DAVID FRECHETTE

AS YOU TRY YOUR BEST NOT TO COMPLAIN

As *YOU* try your best not to complain,
A hacking cough's killing your throat,
Making it tough to sleep or eat.
Your appetite's down, and
You weigh a fraction of your normal size;
Thrush limits the menu anyway.

As you *TRY* your best not to complain,
Lesions and turtle skin compete for leg space.
Your neuropathy's acting up, and
Long walks are definitely out.
You urinate every time you turn
While in constant thralls of constipation.

As you try your *BEST* not to complain,
You're working a night shift
With a couple of nut cases,
Making a fast $300-a-week and no savings at all,
Daring to fantasize about 5-CD rack systems...
If only you could bring your phone bill down!

As you try your best *NOT* to complain,
You've long chucked cruising and disco dancing.
Jet lag affects you in the most eccentric ways;
It's on an itinerary where you travel a lot;
Lately, there are pains you can scarcely mention,
But the X rays failed to turn up anything fatal.

As you try your best not to *COMPLAIN,*
Sometimes the days are mild,
And you actually feel strong.
Friends keep advising Hay and visualization,
But there are some depths all the positive
Thinking in the world can't reach.

THOMAS GLAVE

LANDSCAPE IN BLACK

Is there life after black?

- Advertisement heading, *The New York Times*,
February 16, 1986

If names could hold colors,
the musical notes of you-
as-you-are, named for a saint,
would fill our blackest night skies —

jostling constellations,
elbowing Cassiopeia
for a view of this earth, so dark —
an ancient blackness surrounding you
with the warm dark of tar.

I.

Good News:
All things bad
are not black.

The white lies in your eyes
spill out in black lines.

Red-winged blackbirds
flutter their blackness
in fitful ignorance.

The Atlantic blackens
& blues itself
to the delight of bad artists.

The Brooklyn Bridge
spans all shadows, elegant
in New York light-studded black velvet.

46

We were taught in school
that it is not a color,
but an essence.

It drapes itself
across the backs
of smooth-skinned
delicate women.

It highlights the beauty
of coffee-colored
Black men.

II.

Do you remember
that film about Cambodia
we saw?

That was our time.
I remember

your eyes gleaming black
(dark, expectant
as movie screens),
how your mouth
suckled popcorn

& how your nose,
two black holes, two hairy handles,
ran like a child's.

47

What colors were there!

Villagers in copper tones
singing of desolation,
bloodied orphan children
showing the whites of their eyes.

That night
you told your first lie —
on 6th Avenue, in frigid air
as the stars hung unbelieving
in old heaven-black safety.

Darkness covered us,
taxi exhaust,
poisonous gray fumes.
Do you remember the road's rolling away?
That good black licorice highway....

Where are the ravens
when their warning
is most needed?

III.

There are, for example,
the Following Items:

The arched black back of the wayward alley cat
the black richness of raisins in the thick of plum pudding
the black steel pudenda of a Mercedes-Benz motor
the black pupil circles in my old father's eyes

the black coiled hair on the warm chest of a lover
   black panthers
      & black diamonds &
         5-stud blackjack
            & winter's cold paling over
               black sidewalk cracks

IV.

Do not fear the darkness. Hold it in your hand like a
loathsome spider which has the power to sting you, eat
flies & other vermin, & build six-story cobwebs in the hall
of your mouth. Release it, letting it fall to the floor,
crushing it under your heel until you feel its back breaking.
Wipe away the mess, wash away all blood, & spoon it,
entirely, into the nearest available light. Avoid all shadows
& thoughts of evil. If darkness returns, repeat this
procedure or immediately slice your throat   neatly;
instantly blackness will swallow you. The body will then
decay, returning to light in some other form.

V.   *(Answers to the Dark Questions)*

   (It is black
   just black)

Where does it live?

   In the mouth
   in the black breath
   of the dying addict

Where does it hide?

49

Between the legs
The black void
of starts

What does it do?

Blackens our eyes
dissects our lives
orbits itself

What can we do?

Worship the black
of dead country roads
of crickets in song

Where did it begin?

In the black dead center
the hole of God's ass
the whole of awakening

Where will it end?

In the slums of a city
on a hangman's rope
in a madonna's armpit

VI.   *(Resolution)*

Is there life after black?   If so, where will we find
ourselves as we live it?   At the black dead center, caught
between the pale breaths of our lives & the black lifeline

border? Or in the black belly of a dream, at the abyss
edge of vision? If we are to be saved, who will save us?
The black face of God, peering out from a star's cold eye?

This then believe

    :

        that there is life after black
        the life of the mind

        & thought
        in their spatial leaps
        woven together into the black
        sky tapestry
                            night

        hanging forever over the corners
        of being   this is the black tapestry

    :

        the dark screen
        which nullifies sunsets

        where all stars sink
        & swim like planetary minnows
        like winking forces
        of light

Our lives swim after black. The light of our minds opens
into black. Our bodies lie suspended in light. There is
entry of the soul. (Call it the spirit.) A new blackness

51

awaits us, stirring the dark lifeflow waters... the life
membrane awaits the revision, the clarity and magic....

Welcome the black
the fluid life rush

it will overtake you
the black will overtake you

the world   that too is black
there is the window to our lives

in blackness of night
which is true & black   eternal
as the black whole of awakening
& the black hole of starts
& all our black lovers
revised to clarity
& our lives after black
amniotic
this is the beginning

VII.

I no longer see you

I no longer fear the dark
or the black lies of your eyes

grown malevolent,
glinting,
evil kioshi stones.

Blackness is in my system
& out of it.

Many have thought
of things like this
& come to tell of it.
I am only one.

Darkness hugs me
with its bear-furred arms.

The landscape unfolds,
a black checkerboard,

& the life landscape,
with its black sweet broodings,
hangs back.

Now,
with our eyes agleam
like cats',
our bodies slunk low & cautious,
our arms long & useful,

legs slightly bowed,

we take the first steps
through the gentle blackness
of the game.

ROY GONSALVES

BLACK SUMMER

I know what it's like to pick peppermint
from my garden
to make tea to calm my shattered nerves
wishing for magic to render sanity.

I've torn memories in my photos
ripped decorations by ex-lovers
snipped petunias for fun
burned hate letters in the fire of the grill.
I know what it's like to recite
eighteen psalms in one night
to pray not to become one of Satan's disciples
and cast a deadly spell.

I've heard whispers from my lover's lips
telling me he's sleeping with my so-called friend.
I've lived harlequin romances
and watched them turn into bloody nightmares
where I became a murderer.

I know what it's like to plot murder
to shoot a friend in the face
and watch his smile fall blank
to beat bloody my beloved
with a hammer
and leave him in the cellar.

I know what it's like to choke on hatred
despise the image in the mirror
and every living thing that moves.
I know the terror of being alone
for fear I might kill myself.

I've seen impatiens in my garden
shrivel up and die before my eyes.
I know what it's like to be dead.

I've been to a funeral
in my own home
heard the ancestors scream:
"It's not your time..."
I've watched summer turn black.
I know what it's like to have your heart
turn into hot ice
waiting to burn.

KENTON MICHAEL GREY

JOAN

She moved gracefully from the bathroom to the living room. Her sleek black body shimmered as she passed each long column of sunlight paralleling the hardwood floor. Brazen: The word that befitted her attitude and posture as she stood in one of her picture windows, staring down at the people who walked by. A few looked up to the second floor and smiled. She showed them no emotion. Another pedestrian cast her a friendly wave. She turned then walked to one of the sofas where she lay down on her side.

Her home was huge. She left it only when circumstances forced her. Surrounded by everything she could possibly need, she didn't bother herself with the world. She didn't have to work for her living; who she was saw to that. A manservant to prepare her meals, clean her home, and yes, to provide affection when she was so inclined. He had it made, she would think. He can come and go as he pleases, after taking care of his duties, of course. He got to live in her home, and he had her attention, on occasion, which no man could claim.

She gazed at the gold strip of sunlight falling against the wall, pouring onto the clean wooden floor. Without a thought, she left the sofa, walked to the strip and lay down directly in its beam. Her manservant had left soft music playing for her. Eyes shut, she listened to Billie Holiday sing "She's funny that way," lingering in the sun's warmth.

56

She heard the sounds of her manservant opening the downstairs door. She made no attempt to get up. She rolled on her back, parting her legs so the sun shone directly between them. Desires pure of guilt and shame, her face held the most broad and self-content smile in the world. In her mind, there was no question of her right to lay on the floor if she so wished.

He entered the room and saw her sunbathing. He had seen her like that countless times. She had done things much wilder. Billie Holiday and a saxophone crooned "Embraceable You." He removed his coat, placing it on a nearby chair, then made his way slowly across the room. When he was near, she opened her eyes. He looked directly into them, he too smiling.

"And are we enjoying ourselves?" he asked in a sticky-sweet voice usually reserved for small infants. Then he bent over her, smoothed his hand around her back and lifted her to his right shoulder, cupping her long tail under his left arm. "Did baby miss me?"

She let out a small meow as he rubbed the side of her face. "Is my little girl hungry, huh?" She purred and kneaded at the threads of his sweater with her claws.

"Now, wait a minute, chicky. This sweater cost some serious ducats, go easy on it." He walked toward the kitchen with Joan on his shoulder, petting and cajoling her each step of the way.

MARK HAILE

WHOSE PROBLEM

The son of Martin Luther King, Jr.
Says Gays have a "problem."
He said, quote, "Any man that has a desire
To be with another man has a problem," endquote.

There are a lot of problems that go along
With being a man who desires another man.
Enough problems that we don't need to add
The son of Martin Luther King, Jr. to the list.
Fortunately now, he too has a problem:
He has rightfully heard from us Lesbians and Gays.

And he has insufficiently demonstrated
A change of heart in his sentiments
That would make his parents proud
And pacify our indignation.

CRAIG G. HARRIS

LITTLE GIRLS

I read Lesbian fiction
because on the page
and in my mind
the characters are strong,
pretty, independent,
problem-solving,
and they rarely die

But when I read about boys
most are seropositive
too often pale
and putrid blotches color their faces
They're always ghettoized
in the Castro or Chelsea,
going to therapists
because their daddies
won't let them
bring their lovers home,
or their mamas are dying of cancer,
heartache or shame

There are enough corpses
on my bookshelf,
in my diary,
in my appointment book,
on my Rolodex;
corpses fill my files
of terminated cases,
pending projects,
things I didn't get around to;
cancelled checks to my florist
are stored in a coffin-shaped
box on my desk

But to answer your question:
What do I do to relax?
I read Lesbian fiction
and thank heaven for little girls.

KEITH HARRIS

COME SEE THE MAPPLETHORPE SHOW

THAT'S RIGHT
COME SEE THE MAPPLETHORPE SHOW
COME SEE BLACK MEN
BLACK MEN
COMPOSED AND EXPOSED
FROM THE AMERICAN DREAM

THAT'S RIGHT
COME SEE THE MAPPLETHORPE SHOW
COME SEE BLACK MEN
BLACK MEN
POISED POSED STATUESQUE
WITH SOLID SEAMLESS
BARE CHESTS
IN THE PICTURES
AND AT BEST
OBJECTS
AESTHETICIZED
DE-EROTICIZED
DE-MEMBERED
FROM THE MEMORY
OF MEN MINDS EMOTION
AND HUMANITY

THAT'S RIGHT
COME SEE BLACK MEN
AT THE MAPPLETHORPE SHOW
AND TRY TO FORGET
THE FIRST TIME
YOU MEASURED YOUR DICK

LYLE ASHTON HARRIS

LAST NIGHT I HAD A DREAM

"The search for the object of desire

THAT I WAS BEING FUCKED BY THIS BEAUTIFUL BIG BLACK MAN.

is not governed, therefore, by physiological needs,

HE WAS TALL, DARK AND ROUGH.

but by the relationship to sign or representation.

HE TRIED TO ENTER MY ASS SEVERAL TIMES,

It is the organization of these representations

BUT MY HOLE WAS TOO TIGHT.

that constitutes fantasy.

FINALLY, AFTER MANY UNSUCCESSFUL POSITIONS,

Desire is

HE ORDERED ME TO STAND UP AND ASSUME DOGGY POSITION.

a relationship

HE THRUST HIS DICK INTO ME

to fantasy. "

AND RODE MY TIGHT MANCUNT.

* excerpt from a photo installation: *The Secret Life of a Snow Queen.*

REGINALD HARRIS

SUNDAY MORNING

On days like this, water becomes wine.
The sky's a fault-filled blue,
fluffless clouds skim milk-pale,
weak sun yawns through a scrim haze.
Sunday morning, slow and lazy
from the night before, man to man,
we enjoy each other's body —
your mouth, holy water on my lips.
We look like fresh-baked bread
and taste of pure bee honey.

Later, lounging on the porch,
praise songs drift across the yard.
Orange and pine scents fill our nostrils
as trees echo our last slow dance.
Giant blue-black clouds hover,
then the sky spills forth Chablis.
Everything's a form of prayer,
every act of love a hymn, a gift,
and nothing we do could be sacrilegious
on this perfectly imperfect Sunday morning.

Ashland, Virginia
1982

DRIFTING

You have been wasting a life/
with struggle and strife/
still you wonder/
   late at night/
will the dawn ever come/
the rain stop/
   so you can/
reach out for the light/
and make amends/
   raining again/
will the sun ever shine/
a rainbow will be his sign/

JEFF A. HASKINS

GOSSIP

For the boys who talk a little too much

Lost in idle chatter
Unsung truths from bitter lips
Make-believe stories told
In disloyalty and betrayal
Smite a reputation into debris

Devalue a human being
Belittle a soul floating high
'Cause of a malicious jealousy
Create lies to fill in the empty
Uninteresting spaces of reality

The juicier the better
So everyone who hears will gulp
No shame or guilt do you feel
Carrying out your well-planned
Character assassination

ESSEX HEMPHILL

RIGHTS AND PERMISSIONS

Sometimes I hold
my warm seed
up to my mouth
very close
to my parched lips
and whisper
"I'm sorry,"
before I turn my hand
over the toilet
and listen to the seed
splash into the water.

I rinse what remains
down the drain,
dry my hands —
they return
to their tasks
as if nothing
out of place
has occurred.

I go on being,
wearing my shirts
and trousers,
voting, praying,
paying rent,
pissing in public,
cussing cabs,
fussing with utilities.

What I learn
as age advances,
relentless pillager,
is that we shrink
inside our shirts
and trousers,
or we spread
beyond the seams.
The hair we cherished
disappears.

Sometimes I hold
my warm seed
up to my mouth
and kiss it.

B.MICHAEL HUNTER

WHEN MOMMY BREAKS DOWN

when mommy breaks down
nervous
you scour the bathroom
scrub the floors
wash the windows
do the laundry
dust the living room
change the light bulbs
when they burn out
clean the kitchen
buy the food and cook
for yourself and mommy broken

you walk through the house
quietly
trying to be air
as if the floors were hot coals
broken glass
or a bed of needles

you speak at a volume just right
tone emotionless
watch the news
late-night talk shows
the late movie
listen to the radio
at a volume so low you could hear
mommy's breath in the next room
and you read about history
about triumph
about life

you go to school
on time

late or not at all
but you always do well enough
so mommy would not have
to leave the house
'cause you know mommy shouldn't leave the house
and when she does
you are always by her side
at the bank
(you wonderin' where
she got the check to cash
in the first place)
at the doctor's office
the pharmacy
some relative's house
by her side
always
she needing
to lean

when mommy breaks
you break
into fragments
but if you are to survive
your blood must become glue
'cause you must pull it together

you look into her eyes
around you and guess
guess
if she needs a blanket
something to eat
the tv channel or radio station changed
or it turned on or off
any sign of life

while all the plants in the house die
or try to
but you can't let them
so you take care of them too
you answer the phone
"oh she's not in"
or "oh she'll call you right back"
or "oh she's sleeping"
or "oh she's..."
you leave your friends
at the door
and it doesn't even matter
what you tell them

'cause teenage noise
would certainly disturb mommy
or you
or the stillness
and someone
something should explain
the quiet

"why is mommy..."
who cleaned the house
worked every day
raised four kids
single-handedly while going to college
bought food
gave you and every one
such good advice
"why is she so broken"
so you go through the house
looking for clues

you find papers
you read them all
between and behind every line
you uncover
pictures
books
pieces of the puzzle
secrets
skeletons
and lies

you ask questions
actually you only ask one
at a time
or maybe one a day
or week
or month
'cause you don't want to
wipe away her
surely-to-follow tears

you listen
she tells you everything
a burden lifted
she tells you
'cause you asked
'cause there is no noise in the house
'cause it seems that you and she are
the only living things
and you hear yourself repeating
"it's alright
everything will be alright"

you go to school

join a club
the track team
run in circles
for miles
a natural high
you are good
but you never excel
no
that might mean mommy
would have to talk to the coach
about allowing you to go out of town
to this meet or that meet
then he too might ask why
she doesn't come to a meet
to see how wonderful you are

"you explain things so well
you have so much insight
you're so mature
so thoughtful
so kind
so different" people tell
you thank them all
smile not too wide
'cause even the best glue
won't hold together
if you pull too hard
stretch emotions
too far

unknowingly
your vision becomes narrow
your horizon small
and all you remember is mommy

head bent
shoulders round
sitting in a chair
or on the side of a bed
still
alone
you remember your mother
without you
you think
without you where would she be
what would happen

so you build a wall
a very tall wall
so impregnable
so high no one is able to climb
look over
or get through
it protects you
or traps you
or traps and protects you
it's in your face
your eyes
your mouth
your gait

yet men approach you in the streets
women approach you in the streets
then the streets approach you
you wonder how
everyone and everything know
you need so much
but you never asked for help
you are mommy's
little helper

F. SPENCER IRVIN

BLACK CULTURE IN THE PARK

There's a lot of culture in the park.

From the handsomest B-boys
To the sassiest Divas;
The Black Bourgeoisie
To Homeless America.

There's a lot of culture in the park.

A large wooded area:
A place with fountains and ponds,
Hills and rocks, grass and trees
Where "boys" walk, look, searing,
And men grope, seek, searching
For orgasms.
Do you practice "safe sex"?
Neither did they.

There's a lot of culture in the park.

A young man of twenty-eight or so:
A beautiful man, but a man of the streets —
Survivor — he asked me to pay him
Three bucks, and he'd take care of me.

There's a lot of Black culture in the park...

ISAAC JACKSON

THE ROLE OF THE POET

the role of the poet
is to know when it is going to rain
to keep the parchment dry and cutting

the role of the poet
is to know the difference between quince and apple
to know whether to pick up wildflowers or litter

the role of the poet
is to say the things people think to themselves
but never hear spoken aloud by another person

the role of the poet
is to know when to lift bags of fresh fruits
and vegetables off floors for tables
or when it is better
to take a fender guitar amp up
six flights for rehearsals

the role of the poet
is to be able to taste the difference between
styrofoam and rice cakes
which one gums the mouth and
which one stops the ears

the poet learns how to skin tomatoes
to push back the skin from the head of a penis
when to break bread and invoke the name
of sweet baby jesus
when to peel off a corn husk
fill it with sweet blue jamaican
and sing the songs of bob marley

the poet learns when to smell sweet
when to let perspiration run down
the legs to warm sour fires
of the night

the role of the poet is to know
why the candles shouldn't go out
and when trains will be undependable

the poet keeps secrets and tells lies
knowing what will keep us awake
to keep the fires burning
the scary dreams of the unstoppable
out there in the stars

instead the poet offers us something to
make our lungs collapse
methane perhaps
or some scientific thriller
starring edgar allan poe and karl marx

the poet knows when to rest
where the road is
leaving town

G. WINSTON JAMES

TO BE BRAVE

Can you hear my footsteps as I approach the waiting grave?
Can you see my despair as I descend into death's cave?
Do you recall the day when I imbibed that savage blood?
Do you know of shattered dreams, crushing of frozen rosebud?
How can I look 'round at my prints buried in the deep snow?
How can I bear that as it melts all trace of me will go?
Can you hear my footsteps as I approach the waiting grave?
If so, will you be there with me to help me to be brave?

REDVERS JEANMARIE

HEJIRA

For Yves Lubin

There were no colors
A night without azure
And a cloud-covered moon misted
Our skins
Such yearning could not be pinned
A rustle of trees gave no answers
Nor the ambient air
A sense of plenitude
The road before us with no symbols
A restrictive sense of nothingness
Wrapped us firm
I've a natural strength
And can follow with you
I heard myself
Whisper
Questions long forgotten
What we've become
Has no name

RICHARD E. JENNINGS

HELL
(IN HIGH HEELS)

She laughed as she spat
on the unruly crowd
of wistful admirers.
"All men are created... equal," she
mused while spouting profanity
after profanity.
Little did the perverse
old men
in the audience know that she
was militantly guarding her
virginity.

So her bark was worse than
her bite.

Still she strutted her stuff
across the dimly lit stage,
wearing only lace stockings,
a black garter belt and a
sheer bra that exposed tender
white tits.
Then she sat in a chair
(a mere prop of course),
spread her long legs,
and proceeded to insert
two fingers in her cunt.

She looked like Stalin
in high heels.

She did wear boots on occasion,
like when those kinky CEO's
begged her to step on their balls...
It's all in a day's work to her.
"Hey, it beats working on
Wall Street," she would tell
her lesbian lover(s).
And the strong-arm dykes
loved her hellish charm.
Her cherry is the ultimate
reward in a future life.

She left Kansas for this?
she thought.

Tall buildings, drugs and
fast cars, all were too much
at times for her delicate senses.
So, she thought about the future
And longed to find
the answer —
"Don't you want to find
the answer?" she would ask.
"I just want you, baby,"
her horny lover(s)
responded.

And she believed them; above all
she was naive.

SAMUEL AUGUSTUS JENNINGS

HI-SPEED QUEEN

cruising the corridor
hi-speed queen
metroliner country
upscale scene

civilized shuttle
blazing trails
heavy metal action
sizzling rails

gotham flash
d.c. power
chic connection
on the hour

corporate cult
ticket to success
riding the fastrak
american express

club car clones
sophisticated style
custom service
tailored with a smile

executive training
class on the run
scotch on the rocks
lesson number one

cheaper trains brake
in constant disrepair
metrofones buzzing
recall better fare

no deadheading
passriding taboo
restrictions apply
even to you

yet those excluded
from inside
must subsidize
this royal ride

BRAD JOHNSON

CREW-CUT RECRUIT

ornery beneath a blistering sun,
the barking company
commander breaks discipline
about young heads,

these men bent over sweet
to grab ass in the showers,
all wet-roughened skin and
the darkening eyes to run
you through completely,
recalcitrant in the beauty of
sinewy limbs and the constant
desire to go the distance,

to pull the tongue
across lips of succulence
thick and moist,
with forehead on the warmth
of muscled chest and the sweat
and grasp of hands
in the rack at night's

fulfillment, now touch, now
heave, orgasmic men
in love with the militancy
of love

CARY ALAN JOHNSON

FIRST RAIN IN DAKAR

First rain in Dakar
black skin shines through blue linen
translucent towers run along
streets cursing thanking
God in a village desert no trees to
hold back encroaching sand and nothing
and death waits for small black
children with round bellies women
with small dreams men with equipment
race for coins thrown from moving
cars from wounded men from sallow
women move slow through fields of
new rice fresh with the worms of
irrigation.

SIDNEY CURTIS JOHNSON

SUNDAY, NOVEMBER 6, 1987

He came
like
the day
awakening
color
without
ever
straining
its reason.

* * *

I stared
like
a child
at the circus
awed
with
dim hope
answering
his call.

K. MAURICE JONES

JONES BEACH BATHER

ebony & turquoise ran to greet the sea,
leaping into atlantic coolness.
white tongues dance between black thighs
...sweet salty foam...
washing love muscles
...sweet salty foam...
sucking jewels
...sweet salty foam...
swimming over mountains
...sweet salty foam...
plunging into valleys
neptune's children baptizing the blues,
a black bather reborn.
outstretched arms touch the sky.

ANTHONY B. KNIGHT-DEWEY

LONELINESS

Loneliness is an abandoned house. It creaks
with stillness and rests
on the blackness of its foundation.
It sits alone in the backyard of our minds, yet stands
out and demands recognition. It hides elusively
behind the rubbish of life, yet shines a light most
radiant from its highest loft.
It is weather-beaten from years of torment
and anguish, but still retains its shape and strength.

Loneliness gives no clues or suggestions.
Secrets are hidden and locked away in the attic of
darkness. Groans and cries race
through the pitted corridor
down the infested stairwell to the moldy basement.

Loneliness gathers dust in the dungeon of time.
The windows of hope and aspiration are boarded up
with the grayness of despair.

Yet, only in loneliness does one experience all those
dimensions that are one,
those distant faraway lands of beingness —
the spirit supreme,
the temple eternal.

STEVE LANGLEY

BUTCH

My name Butch
I work at the hardware store
I got this lil gal I be messin wif
Fine as shit
She wanna move in wif me
But I don't need no bitch up under me
Wantin this and that
I be hangin out at this punk club
Somethin to do
I may get a drink, get high
But I don't talk to nobody
If I do hook wif somebody
I go to they place
I may let em suck my dick
I may fuck em
But I don't be kissin em
And they bet not try to kiss me
I'll beat the shit out of em
I don't give em my name or my number
Not my real one
Once I git off
I'm gone

CEDRIC LEVON

HAIKU

wax candle drippings
like lovers' seeds on my chest
they cool just the same

JOSEPH LONG

THERE ARE NO POEMS
FOR AFRICAN AMERICANS

WHEN WE SPEAK TRUTHS
OUR OPPRESSORS REFUSE TO LISTEN
MELODIC WORDS CHOKE UP IN OUR THROATS
DON'T EVEN BECOME WHISPERS
THEY TRICKLE BACK DOWN OUR WINDPIPES
CUT OFF OUR OXYGEN SUPPLY
THEY BLIND US WITH STIFLING RAGE
EAT AWAY AT OUR FLESH
FESTER LIKE SORES ALL OVER OUR SKIN
BRANDED BY LABELS
SHACKLED BY HANDCUFFS
SEDATED BY DRUGS AND RELIGION
THESE UNFORMED DEFORMED POEMS CAUSE US
TO LEAVE THIS WORLD
TEN YEARS BEFORE OUR TIME
OR THEY SIMPLY DIE BEFORE THEY ARE BORN
THERE ARE NO POEMS FOR AFRICAN AMERICANS

HARVEY J. LUCAS

TOO LATE TO SAY I LOVE YOU

For David

Often he was parental,
But the rebellious pride masked
His contentment with concern.

Often he was great,
Generic in dress — forceful passion —
And a dynamic friend.

Often he was risqué,
Public kisses — arrogant smirks —
Not afraid to say anything.

Now, I often remember him:
Consumed by that inscrutable entity
Of eternal silence.

JEROME MACK

FLAW

Sometimes
i wish i could
rid myself
of this skin
that covers me
subdue carnality
pick fights
with truth
pull husk
over conscience
i would...
there's just no
hiding place

SCOTT MACKEY

I COULDN'T SPEAK HIS LANGUAGE

For Romuald Du Clos de Saint André

when i first met him,
he was only a boy,

but not really.

he allowed me to believe
i was in control — the man,
old, wise and mature.

reality obscured the dream
because
i couldn't speak his language.

he knew
but needed to hear
what i couldn't say.

a part of me burns
as i become
desperately aware of my mortality.

i didn't realize

how important,
words could be.

VERNON MAULSBY

GENDER BENDER

To Richard

Is it safe for me
to let my hair down
and speak freely with you?
Will this woman's heart
speaking through a deep throat
make you dismiss me
as just another gender bender,
incomplete in your eyes?
Can I share the men I've loved,
the women I've liked, the fears
of death that sired my children?
Would you understand,
or should I just sit here,
and make lewd jokes, as we
talk of sports I never watch?

RODNEY MCCOY, JR.

POP

I used to dream
of a ghost in
silk
satin
lace

Dreaming of
gold
tightening around
my finger
like a blessing
or was it a noose

These dreams
were my mother's smile
handed down
to my sister
and me
thinking it was
our birthright
our duty
our gift to her

But the day I kissed
your mustached lips
silk
satin
lace
to me

Those dreams
and my mother's smile
popped loud
painful
absent forever

BOB MCNEIL

SERVING MAN

...In the twilight of clarity
The family gathers 'round.
　　Moments stagger
With wooden-leg grace;
　　Mendacity permeates the air.
In them,
　　I see seven sins
Roll their tongues over the prospect
　　Of a confrontation,
Smack lips over old grievances,
　　Lick open
Festering wounds
　　And savor pain —
The last morsel.
　　No one seems to realize
We are devouring ourselves
　　And at once
My hope
　　Falls to the whirling floor —
When, with compassion,
　　We could be saved.
My naive axiom:
　　An uninvited guest
At the human dinner table.

METAPHORA

POEM FOR THE CLUB KIDS

for the young divine deluxe queens
with grand affectations
house music working magic
in your fingers that ferociously snap
and legs that kickbox with flair

for the snaps
that don't give a fuck
about phobic stares
from errant irrelevants
(people?) traveling southward
on the west side highway
ogling at the christopher st. zoo

for the polka dots
and the piers
and the kente cloth
and the bright colors
and the big straw hats
and the sandals
and the purses
and the highest
hosanna-in-the-highest
most-empowered high top fades

don't let them tell you what you are
or what you ain't
fierceness is an obliterating stratagem
you are the light-bearing post-stonewall divas

ALAN E. MILLER

EVERYWHERE THERE'S EVIDENCE

Everywhere
there's evidence
I'm prepared
for any emergency

in the bedroom:
a flashlight,
Swiss Army knife,
battery-operated watch-radio,
a deck of cards,
condoms

in the bathroom:
enough floss to last 'til the afterlife,
deodorant and vitamins,
birth control pills for my plants,
several portable mirrors

in the pantry
just essentials:
a case of wine,
a dozen cans of tuna,
a portable stove,
a can of RAID

in the kitchen:
several rows of bottled water
beneath the sink,
a box of matches,
one hundred candles,
my heart, dangerous
as a bone in my throat —

yes, I'm ready —
earthquake,
nuclear attack,
sudden loss of power —

I'm ready —
for all but this:
you, black moth,
masquerading as a butterfly

JIM MURRELL

BERMUDA

Fine.
Hot.
Luminous.
Infinite carapace of day ingathers hard, riding noon fire
On molten hillocks beyond the coral.
Sun-drovered come
Sarabands of iodine, nomad across the sea grape.
Pupils burn to pinpoint smoke: rolling glitter of
Water's desert.
Our boat burns in rise and slap
And indigo swells from the east:
My father, the friends of his youth, myself.

And I am thirteen, struggling to man manliness.
Head, heart, stomach... vortex.
Resolve eddies on fuming wash of clubbed fish blood.
Betrayal of inner ear for which gravity is not enough.
And the rum talk: pompous, monotonous.
Men and ritual braiding the deep world into submission —
Pattern of a weaving,
A harnessing I cannot learn.

JOHN S. PATTERSON

HOW IT FEELS WHEN YOU FALL ON YOUR HEAD IN LOVE

For Sean

Do you mind
If the next time you kiss me

I just fall out for four or five seconds.

Your kiss is meditation
And I want to go

OMMMMMMMMMMMMMMMMMMMMMMMMMMMMM

All night long.

To contemplate:

Your six-feet-six of Olympian sweetness.

To contemplate:

That manly tangle of arms and legs anarmsanlegsanarmslegsarms...

To contemplate:

My home in this rock.

So do you mind,
If
The next time you kiss me
I just fall out for four or five seconds.

Your kiss is meditation
And I want to go
OMMMMMMMMMMMMMMMMMMMMMMMMMMMMM

All
Night
Long.

REGINALD PATTERSON

TIME
(BE STILL)

For Allen Wright

the moments fly when i am in his embrace
time, be still
show me no wicked clocks or hourglass sand
i want no ticking in my life
i beg you time be still, let his arms
hold me for infinity
let his hands grope, never find the source
of my deepest ecstasy
let him listen, forever wait to hear the most
beautiful words I can say
let him search my eyes, never know an end
to his searching
be still,
be still, time
imprison us in ecstatic infinity

ROBERT E. PENN

HECKLERS' FEAR

I don't think I'll wear makeup
Pancake over lesions
It's too difficult to match
The warmth of my color
Too deceitful to hide a
      manifestation.

So easy for the "unaffected"
To point fingers
My beard may conceal spots
But does nothing to soothe
      hecklers' fear
They must cope with what they see.

ELEO POMARE

ELEGY FOR A SCHOOLMATE

Our desks were
connected
side by side.
YOU
exposed yourself
to me
during homeroom,
satisfied yourself
while you called me names
and begged me
to touch
YOU.

How were we to know
that ten years
later,
cradled in my arms,
you would beg me again,
this time for you to stroke
ME?
I asked then took you
to buy jelly donuts
and honey dipped in coffee
on your acid trip.

Oh Jim,
for your madness,
for unspeakable despair
for which I forgave you.
You have now taken yourself
away,
far from the tea shop

across Washington Square Park,
from our room
where I held you, protecting
you from you,
every muscle taut,
shivering in the dark,
tense.

The room,
its walls blind,
is silent now.
The things that in passing
you left behind
will never feel your caress.
The pillow you left on your bed
has lost the imprint of your head,
plants in the window always seem
to grow but not to bloom.

Feeling frayed,
was I not honest in friendship?
Betrayed,
knowing
this was your trip,
with its middles
beginnings and end;
your living tapestry,
threads,
stitches of human tailoring,
not my shame,

Your
sacrificial solitude.

CHARLES R. P. POUNCY

BUDDY

Daddy asked why
I was still alone at 35
shook his head
held his glasses
loosely in sharecropper's hands
said I was too choosey
I said I can't take
another sissy dressed in black
another diva sans portfolio
with drop earrings and razor nails
another weave
another curl
another tail
another 40-year-old boy
another grand attitude
another bergman/fellini/fassbinder discussion
over smelly brie and bitter champagne
Daddy smiled
squinted thru the damp air

I want someone who is objectively male
not the guerrilla warrior
shopping at saks
the pinocchio shoes pointing nowhere
the black "skin and bones" bette davis with a dick
the hand forced against a collapsing spine
the hollow cackle
the lizard strut
I can't take another room
crammed with old wood and ugly dogs
I won't eat another chicken wing
off a silver tray
I won't sit on another couch
covered with a dead cow

I want to say
Daddy this is the man in my life
and not have you say
the what
Daddy cleared his throat roughly
said he wouldn't say that
I said I know but
it's not in me anymore
it's not fun anymore
there's no hope anymore
I don't want to be gay
anymore

Daddy asked if I had made a mistake
I said no
I just want a man
who shops at sears twice a year every year
who slaps me on the back when he laughs
who gets up early on saturday mornings
who drinks manischewitz for medicinal purposes
who plays checkers when the fish aren't biting
who wants children
who holds my hand in daylight
who prays in church on sundays
a man like you
Daddy shook his head
ran his hand across the moistness
under his eyes

CRAIG A. REYNOLDS

THE MOON SINGERS

The Darbat, Cheyenne, Yoruba and Eskimos,
interpreting the seizures I had as a child,
would have welcomed me as a shaman, a wanderer in the wild.
Living with the women, I,
      hairy-faced like you, would have worn their clothes.
One day, I would journey to find
      the familiar who'd name me, help
me to heal, and teach me to talk with omen
birds unknown even to the tribe's best bowmen.
This done, I would return to our wolf-clan's greeting yelp.

But, in this advanced civilization,
I have neither name nor habitation.
So you and I, in self-initiation,
should adorn ourselves with ostrich plumes dyed bloody maroon,
paint our faces the blue of the mandrill baboon,
and dance the fertility frenzy for the full-bellied moon.

L. PHILLIP RICHARDSON

THE BOOK OF LISTS

so fickle ink on first acquaintance
i penciled them in
the urban gods
the fleeting sparkles
the would-be stars
were the heavens kinder those days

by name i now browse the list
the ABC's of ruthless order
unordered by homeless strays
the innumerable nicknames
attached to numbers
on unattached slips of paper
at home in my book
like family

i remember the first call
in my ear the first word
high on "hi"
the voice vibrating man vibes
then the jittery jive
of jigsaw sympathies
the flirts
the dirts
the jerks
the hurts
still hurting

suddenly i see
the old book older
its frayed memories losing the fray
as some fall free
come loose without restraint
no spine
no rubber binds them
holds them close

i chill
with each name i can't erase
how graceless and cheap faint recall
leaving dead men in leaded glory
in the book of lists
i keep

COLIN M. ROBINSON

HORIZONTAL STRIPES ARE IN
(a fashion advisory from the Marike de Klerk Spring Collection)

"...Aries... My best friend's an Aries too. I really like Aries people.
So tell me: what's your antibody?"

Post the minus sign
mezuza on your doorway
Let it dangle golden
from your ankle
like a southern chain
Strap it to your forehead like a frontlet
pressing on the brain
Or wrap it round your wrist in bondage
like your name
Weave it into charms
and scratch it into crystals
Shop for buttons
baubles
Hang it
in a collar on your neck
Tattoo a tiny straight cicatrix
on your cheek or
asshole skin back
display your modern cut
To overstate it shave a line into your bush

Wear it like I've worn my sexual choices
Parade it proudly
Flaunt it like a man
Put it in your CV on your ID in the phone book
Don't forget to stamp it on your mail
Think negative
Be testy

Horizontal stripes are in

HAROLD MCNEIL ROBINSON

THE VALE OF KASHMIR

In Prospect Park
four paths lead down
to a brick walkway
encircling a watery crescent
fed by spring
Secluded by tiers of trees and bushes
ripples in that pond
reflect a strong and eastern light
as a pool in any oriental garden might
Stone steps lead on
to an upper pathway
where so many men have walked
in search of sex and affection

Olive pants and jeans
pulled below their knees
atop sneakers and combat boots
two men on a park bench
suck each other down
to nappy pubic hairs
not a condom in sight
as they shake and spasm

Months later
a morning sandstorm
leaves a powdery residue
on every surface inside a tent
pitched among endless mountains
of surreal dunes
somewhere near the Kuwaiti border
While eating reserve-unit rations
one of the men

reads a letter from the other
fighting infection
in a hospital
back in Brooklyn
Then noticing grains of sand
even in the envelope
this soldier in the desert
so far away from the pool
of the Vale of Kashmir
wonders which war will come first

PHILIP ROBINSON

WE STILL LEAVE A LEGACY

To United Spirits*

Each death chisels away at my life; no other impact has entered as
strongly....
Now, no cries can go unheard.
There is a newer purpose to these days; in fact, the aftermath tends to
linger longer this time, allowing lives to be reassessed.
We have become more in touch with our own mortality.
Revelations are meaningful timetables to this discovery.
Those who die in silence often experience more pain.
To bury one's dreams is to let go of life; our mission, a larger mission, is
to complete tasks left incomplete....
Our greatest weapon against fear will be the collective intelligence and love
willed to us through our higher power....
When the deepest of emotions have been put in check; we will have acquired the sense of
touching and caring for ourselves; sources of true deliverance.
The enforced censorship of private affairs will never censor my love, our love, the
movement....
There are beams of hope, and faith directs us, keeping the searching infinite....
This is one battle we'll win.
We have been handed the torch; our march is for us, is for them, is forever....

*Taken from "We Still Leave a Legacy";
A part of The Names Project Quilt (1988)

115

ASSOTO SAINT

HEART & SOUL

To Essex Hemphill

every day
every time i leave my house
everywhere i go
i pin on my knapsack
twin petal-small flags
to which my allegiance is pledged
whole

these flags are not monkeys on my back
i carry them as a coat of arms
mantles of double brotherhood
they shield like second skin
to drape my dreams

one floats rainbow
the other wings tricolor
both bold with movement
i am not ashamed
of what they stand for
when their meaning is
questioned

these flags are not chips on my shoulders
i carry them as beauty spots
markings of double brotherhood
they shine like mirror beads
to reflect prejudice

one unfurls the future of queers
the other salutes african ancestors
both wave s.o.s. signals
i am not afraid
to stand my ground
when their beauty is
challenged

> *these flags are not crossbones on my life*
> *i carry them as amulets*
> *emblems of double brotherhood*
> *they spellbind like stars*
> *to stripe america*

glory
that becomes me in tribal rituals
& battle against bigots
i have honored with my blood
everywhere i go
every time i leave my house
every day

BRYAN SCOTT

ROLLER COASTER

You've called but haven't spoken.
You've expressed but haven't clearly stated.
You've suggested but haven't taken action.
You've reached out but haven't connected.
You've touched but haven't felt.
You've been here yet you seemed elsewhere.
You've mentioned "love" but implied "like."
Before I get on this emotional roller coaster
I'd better listen to the silence...

CARLOS SEGURA

CLASSIFIEDS

wanted
a man
to hold me
during thunderstorms
so i won't shiver anymore
fuck
through blizzards
so i could keep warm

white men need not apply

knowledge of snap-finger theories
girlfriend language
or cha-cha queenologies
need not apply

philosophies of
bebopism
dick holdism
or home boy talkism
not required

occupation a must
kissing a must

he needs to know
and be comfortable
with him

wanted
a man
who will sit between my legs
describe his dreams

lay beside me
tell me he's afraid
cry

it'd be fun if he were ticklish

one
who will come home
to our apartment
throw his bag
his coat
across the room
and me
on our overstuffed sofa

forget about
nine to five
white people
black people
miss things
got mugged
raped
evicted
fired
bashed
pop finger
bullshit
every day
and kiss me down

one who will want
me
love
me

applications being considered

GABRIEL SIMS

3 A.M.

Me and John
  Stand outside
His four-wheel truck,
  Smoke dope,
  Drink cheap beer.
  In the moonlight,
The lake smiles—
  Reflects distant downtown
  Reflects the lights from
  Townhouses.
    Feeling warm summer winds
We listen to Marvin Gaye
  Sing of waited love.

NEIL SIMS

BUSHMASTER

One day you will go
Too far
Over the edge
Of this shrinking world.

Can you hear
Jívaro warnings   Surucucu
Jararaca
Cascabela muda?

Can you feel
Your shrunken head
No bigger
Than your tight little fist?

JAMEZ L. SMITH

DREADED VISITATION

For my Grandmother

The knock on the door
on the lazy Saturday afternoon
comes
like the toll of Donne's bell.
Someone runs
and turns the television off.
The air becomes as still
as a dead fish.
Slowly, carefully,
Grandmama tips toward the window.
Another knock breaks
the silence,
and Grandmama freezes
like a doe suddenly aware
of the hunters stalking her.
Finally,
Grandmama reaches the window
and, recognizing the form outside,
breathes a sigh of relief.
She opens the door.
"What took you so long?"
the visitor asks.
Grandmama replies
"We thought you was a Jehovah's Witness."

SUR RODNEY (SUR)

I'M LOST
IF-FOR-WANTING-MY-DREAMS-LESS-YOUR-HEAT

My lover, when
(the triggered noise)
you drive me through madness.
By you I'm exploded
flowering (stiff) concern for
excitement/my lover
excitement: when
I started to feel
the lingering of
my hand: some feeling
my horse: deep breathing
my dreams: moments of our next day.

I've projected
(focus withstanding)
our present-passing.
Realized illusions shattered
within moments of clearer vision
Triggered, when
I explode: long, stemmed passions.
I'm devoting this letter: driven through your madness.

I go into dreams (floated at your side)
loving your waves.
My finger tips surface.
your armor (my wonder) lightly bronzed.
Life has our madness.
You read literature
your spirit my joy.
Deep in desire
my love reveals
fired: love conceals (when)
I'm lost if-for-wanting-my-dreams-less-your-heat.

124

RODGER TAYLOR

THE PERFORMANCE

Huddled in his darkened corner of the cage, the ancient infant hides another tear by willing it to cling to the duct until evaporation leaves only a small stain. Later, when no one is watching, he'll raise a finger to remove the smudge.

Suspended in midair, scarcely moving, curled about himself in womb-like tranquility, oh how he fascinates the spectators. Their anticipation grows as they await the special moment when the centuries-old child creates the only sound he has ever made. There is breath-held silence as the Conductor raises his arm for the signal.

They do not know that his eyes stay shut because he believes the harsh light would blind him. They do not know that he is afraid to touch the hard earth. If his urine flowed, what of him would remain? Even the thought of taking a chance is risky. And *their* attention!

The Conductor lowers his arm, and the crowd intones in unison: "I Love You..."

The silly giggle of the old child jiggles through the cage as he wills, yet another tear.

TERENCE TAYLOR

CIRCLE JERKS

1.
I want them, but they want him.
Beautiful brown, beige and blue
Blacks pass me by, flow around
Brush close, smile, whisper
Reminders of past encounters
Dashing hopes.

2.
They want him, but he wants me.
The texture of my hair
The shade of my skin
To hide his oppression in mine
To overshadow his fears
With my darkness.

3.
He wants me, but I want them.
Black mouths suck only teeth
As he pins me in his headlights
I stare him down
Cold rage in my eyes
Ice in my heart.

6.
He wants me, but I want them.
Will, worn thin as my Levis
Hating them for hating me
Hating him for hating himself
Hating myself for hating it all
At last call, I surrender.

5.
They want him, but he wants me.
Because I don't want him
Pain yearns in his eyes
Fingers dance on his glass
Rejection nearly as satisfying
As my submission.

4.
I want them, but they want him.
The pale silk of his skin
The touch of long blond bangs
Against their necks in the night
Contempt for conquered lands
Stays conquistador hands.

DUNCAN E. TEAGUE

IN THE BACKYARD FOR WALTER
(OR OUR FRIED CHICKEN CUSTOMS)

I absolutely love chicken on paper plates
In hot backyards
After a good funeral 'round Labor Day time
Women — dignified, cultured, bronzed to Black —
Sitting in circles around the serving table
Men in the shade, dressed up like
    Rev. Williams on first Sunday
In white cotton ironed shirts
And colorful ties, sweating
I'm glad our city ways have not taken a good backyard
    Funeral dinner from us
We've never needed that much money
    To be this classy
    To have this much fun
    To honor one so festive
As though Walter was there
    I know I heard "Child, stop!" in the seldom warm
    Breeze behind some funny remark
We taled the tale
From the soul, we laughed the life energy
We loved our own through the hurt
    The real hurt
It is healing to know
    I will drop in on backyard chicken dinners
    Laughing with my "family"
    On my way to Walter's new place

ULYSSES

HOW WHITE FOLKS LEARN ABOUT US
(OR HOW INTEGRATION TEACHES US
ABOUT OURSELVES)

With biting bitterness,
I battled Huckleberry Finn.
Through gritted teeth,
I took my time to read Jim's lines
In class,
Aloud.

I was an innocent child, a sensitive child.
My British teacher acclaimed this book a classic.
"You should be proud... Now read (aloud)!"

As my white classmates all mocked and laughed,
Mocked and laughed, aloud...
"Yes'm Ah's sho' beez prawd."

No Langston Hughes,
No Frederick Douglass,
Not even Imhotep,
For this sensitive lil Negro child

Just (Nigger) Jim...
And mo' proof the Negro has always been just a mass
O' po' pitiful people.

Nameless, faceless, aimless man-apes
In a white man's world.

"You should be proud,"
She had spoken through clear blue eyes.

"Yes'm Ah's sho' beez prawd."

129

VEGA

VOICE PALS

For D. Freeman

We have talked
on the phone,
several times now.
Even though
we have never met,
I feel
that I know you.

The softness of your voice
like a melody
in my mind,
soothing,
captivating,
motivates
a rush to my senses.

After a day of turmoil,
when we talk,
hours at a time,
I feel relaxed,
strong,
courageous —
a welcome treat.

I have never known anyone
to hold me completely
by the timbre of voice
with honesty,
sincerity,
intelligence,
and yes, intrigue.

I cannot remember the last time
that I laughed
at a joke,
at myself,
or the world
with such convictions.
You have enriched my life.

Already you have taught me
so many things:
Trust,
friendship,
compassion,
especially what I want
from you.

I am almost afraid to meet you
face to face,
the tension,
confusion,
the hope of dreams
yet realized
for fear of love.

RICHARD WASHINGTON, JR.

IN FIVE-POUND CORDOVANS

Heart beating in my ears
I rubbed the sweat of my hands
On my knees
A hand reached out
Pale and dry
Bordered by cotton and flannel

In suburban voice
I was told
"Thanks for your time
We'll call you real soon, son"
He called me *Son*

Door closing behind me
I sweat
And exhume a quivering sigh
Remove my specs
Pocket square my brow

Here I am
In five-pound cordovans
Condensed onto a plane
Looking to shine
Subtlety the order of the day

Nina sings
"To be young, gifted and Black"
Sweet Sister
It ain't so easy
When your time has
Passed

DAVID WATTS

LIBIDO/ALBEDO

The moon, most say,
Is a feminine symbol,
But we assert
It sheds a virile light.
It shines for the lover,
          Red starflower in his heart
Flexing in its ambition.
White light gives back all the rays it is.
The dark, its absence, accepts them all.
You came to me,
Offering love
          With a torque in it,
And I took its every twist.
We embraced,
One belly, one thought.
Only in the wild minds of the lonely
Does fancy burn more brightly:
Our passion knows no gender.

DAVID WEEMS

TRADE TALK CAN'T HURT

met him tuesday
workin'
hot, hard but fragile
as ice in july
temporary
we walked
talked in circles
both in need
wantin'
he, shelter
food
cash
i, some rap
stiff cock
(we settle for pizza)
time passes
the night is cold
i think of him
not much different
than me
two days later
he calls
we meet
i bring him a sandwich
he dicks me!!
i've learned
trade talk can't hurt

ROBERT WESTLEY

WHAT'S HAPPENING

It is not necessary to wait long
To see it happen —
Happening in the streets
Red with black blood
Happening in hallways
Littered with semen stains
Happening behind doors
Where babies loll on the floor
Scream with pain and tear each other's hair.
It's happening right now.
A young girl surrenders her secrets
To the boy she loves, but
When they rise from her bed
Nothing remains between the sheets but
Vaginal secretions, some dark decaying spit
No love and not even a condom.
Everything she will know of him is inside her now
Her bones are light beams
Her arms are wings
And if the bedroom window won't do for a fall
The butcher knife is in the kitchen drawer.
It's happening.
Happening, by the way, in your neighborhood
You of the fresh-dew flowers
You of the scornful looks who hide
Behind your money it's pulled
Not just your petty crimes
Like murder or theft
A simple toke on some smoke or coke
Cheap sins that wash off on Sunday
Someone's abusing your mind
Fucking your son

Deceiving your daughter
Filling your house with shit
As if I care
You could take the dare
End the affair
Eat a pear
Turn to prayer
Stare into reality like a basin
Full of heavy water
And cleanse your skin
Of the evil that's within
But forget it.
You are not what's happening.

MARVIN K. WHITE

LAST RIGHTS

When I learned of Gregory's death
I cried silently
But at the funeral
Giiiiirl I'm telling you
I rocked Miss Church
Hell I fell to my knees twice
Before I reached my seat
Three people had to carry me
To my pew
I swayed and swooned
Blew my nose
On any and every available sleeve
The snot was flying everywhere
Then when I finally saw his body
My body jerked itself
Right inside that casket
And when I placed my lips on his
Honey the place was shaking
I returned to my seat
But not before passing by his mother
Who I'm sure at this point
Was through with me
I threw myself on her knees
Shouting "Help me
Help me Jesus"
When someone in the choir
Sang out "Work it girl
Wooooork it"
All hell broke loose
I was carried out
Kicking and screaming
Ushered into the waiting limo

Which sped me to his family's house
Where I feasted
On fried chicken
Hot water corn bread
Macaroni and cheese
Johnny Walker Black
Finally in my rightful place

MICHAEL WIGGINS

MOSAIC CHILDREN

in the ruins of for god so loved the world
i stand on my toes
to kiss your lips
in the middle of seventh avenue

sing the little boy electric blues
to the silver convertible moon
takes the sky
like a freeway of black tar
refrains bend the night
like a tube of heated glass
i pirouette
i ask
what kind of soul am i
have slain a phone book full of men
in the backroom battlefields of god bless america
i learned to dance at the end of the world
what kind of soul am i
coveting your box of tomes and artifacts
your mother's wedding band becomes
a cockring in my hands
deny my history
i will deny you yours

i will become whosoever believing in you
and your two-dollar everlasting candles
burn
as we draw two crooked lines well into morning
with your hand as a bracelet
we two mosaic children
cannot speak
even when spoken to

even if you should put the clock back in its place
say stay
and climb
        down into
                        me
if you should speak
no be silent
be cuneiform
press your name into the wet clay of my night
use only those signs of life we share
nothing but each other
and then grudgingly i fear
someday i will look for you
sliding through subway trains
between the pages of a book
on the cluttered floor of my desires
shall follow me into the apocalypse
when stones rise up like men
and speak your name.

BOB WILLIAMS

THEM BOYS IN BUBBA'S BAHBA SHOP

Some come from 'cross town; others just 'round —
Them boys in Bubba's Bahba Shop.

Long ones, short ones, fat ones too;
Coal-toned, red-toned, saffron hues;
Brown eyes, black eyes, sea-green blue;
Loud ones, quiet ones: all with views.

Some come from 'cross town; others just 'round —
Them boys waitin' to get locks chopped.

JOHN D. WILLIAMS

brother malcolm:
malcolm x speaks to history

father allah —

    i do not understand.

    self-repeating idiocies inundate
    the walls of this place
    like the confines of the sea.

    human history blurs
    in repetitions of murder:
    bodies transgress the land
    like fallen elms.

    there must be a place
    where the language does not lift
    and peel from the senses
    like newspaper in the streets
    on a windy day.

    the disdain for human life
    is painted across the memory
    in bright relief —
    the human being is effaced
    in the transcription of wounds.

    waterways in disuse burnish the face.

ARTHUR T. WILSON

ONE RAWDOG NIGHT
WHEN TOO MUCH OF MY QUEER
WAS SHOWING

It's so hard to breathe,
To dance inside a nightmare life
   Of desperation
   And come-often tears.
What happens to our Prayers?
I scream. I holler. I fall apart.
And there's no one there.
O where's my lawyer? My Mother?
A friend?

Officers,
I'm not some cheap two-bit whore.
I just want to LIVE
And be introduced to kindness.
ANYBODY? Please, listen to me.

One rawdog night
When too much of my queer
Was showing,
Each bone-bruising hurt,
Each humiliation
Had nothing to do with my hemline
   Hanging out of place,
   Or my panties showing.

It all started in the same old way,
ME standing on the corner.
Hey There MISTER. REACH OUT!
Reach out! Take a Sweet Trip to Paradise.
O come on,

Touch me gently. I'm lonely.
Frightened, but being real REAL.
There are lumps in my throat,
   And I'm bursting inside.
   Lost in frayed dreams,
   Evicted again. Too much traffic
The LANDLORD SAID,
   Nine months back in rent
And all my money spent.

Home gone.
Love dry.
   Where was my next bed?
   I try not to cry
   But the tears speed out —
   AND I wonder who would steal
      My roach-filled couch?

What? No! I'm... I'm not a Thief.
Not on the game Sucker.
Well, fuck off! Creep.
What's a girl to do? Hello, YOU... gently.

O that Night,
There I was, again, neglecting myself,
Needing to be comforted,
Leaning, I mean REALLY LEANING
Up against yet another life gone
AND rancid ghetto hole:
A nasty tenement building

Where junkies leave their needles
And ceaseless homicide rings
On the window ledge.
I was leaning, and the building was leaning
Into the entrapment of its own devastating neglect.

Leaning
Drunk, I met a man.
His name was Blue, he said.
He smiled, searched for his keys
And fell up the steps of grief.
Too much booze, drugs and wrong-way living
On mean streets.
        As Blue began spitting out
        The wreckage of yesterday's
        Bitter regrets,
I told him that's the only kind of day that I get.
But I don't be wallowing in no SOUR GRAPES —
I WALK WITH PRIDE,
AND I DECLARE MY SPACE!

Clearly, I knew who I was.
I had to go on living,
Practicing no closed doors,
        Giving.
Believe me, OFFICER, I had to ride
The monkey out,
Be with Blue. I was tired and I needed a bed.

Blue rolled them big brown gone eyes
At me and began to apologize,
Embarrassed to take me inside.

146

Said he'd lived there all his life.
In that last moonlight spilling,
He cried. Sobbing deep and wide and full out,
Blue cried and cried.
So a man's tears rolled down my shoulders,
        Hands making me hot,
        Grasping and feeling my thighs.
But, I too,
        That next morning,
        Barely hanging on,
        Had big hurt,
        Big hurt inside.
        No laughter
        But didn't curse my Birth.

There were runs, runs in my stockings,
And yes, I did care.
A strange tiny spirit was fighting
To keep a song of hope in my heart,
        But I wondered
        How could Blue
        Help me touch the sky.
Then I thought to myself,
Suppose Blue
Became another letdown,
Like my afternoon graveyard piece.

FLASHBACK MEMORIES.
The sun was glaring.
Hot wool dress.
INDIFFERENCE AND ICE.
Hard life. Few friends.

No place to go,
And those times that no one calls.
    Standing on the corner,
    I still had to make a few dollars.
    Then this Vincent PHONEY strolls by.
    Tired eggs but I needed the bacon.

Everything happened so fast.
He's obnoxious
And in love with the superman ego
    Of his own fiction
    That he puffs like a viper.

We're at the door.
He shuts the shades quickly.
The drinks are poured.
Before I can wet my lips,
Elmer Fudd is on me like a ton,
Mauling my ears. Amyl nitrate.
My dress is raised.
A grizzly noodle like putty moves
Across my chest.
He claws. He nuzzles. And it's OVER;
I'm barely wet.

The CRETIN pops up like a bad dream.
HOW ARE YOU DOIN', he says.
DULLED OUT, I say.
But he doesn't understand.
He goes to the bathroom,
Throws me a funky cold washcloth.
WHEN CAN I SEE YOU AGAIN? IT WAS

FABULOUS.
FABULOUS. He gives me three dollars.
It's his last he says. DO YOU LIKE CHEESE
SANDWICHES?
I just pulled down my dress,
And split
Back to Blue.

Then Blue suddenly started bleeding.
And the blood was rushing out of his mouth.
Hemorrhage.
O shit!
I screamed and SCREAMED.
          Everybody heard me
          But responded like ghost-town inhabitants.
          My brains playing tricks on me?

Four Peter Heads
In an old car came careening around the corner,
Willing to share all their nasty years
Of frustration and poison.
Please help me. The car skids. He's BLEEDING.
The men laughed, cursed me horrible names,
But I'm used to all of that.
YOU KILLED YOUR FAGGOT PARTNER
AND STILL TRYING TO GET SOME HEAD,
That's what they
Officers said.

God damn it!
I was so fucking angry. Blue needed a hospital.
I couldn't tie a tourniquet around his mouth.

So my ghetto Prince with the big brown gone eyes
Became a canvas of blood under the sunset.
And then the car,
The car BACKED UP fast and furious —
GUN SHOTS...

Bullets ricocheted across a concrete hell.
One bullet straight through Blue's head
And one bullet into my left arm.
I DIDN'T KILL BLUE. I DIDN'T. I DIDN'T!
Please, don't hit me in the head.
Hit me any other way you choose, but PLEASE
Don't hit me in the head!

Then the Bastards jumped out of the car.
They grabbed me. Hurt me. I remember
Faces moving behind the shades
And curtains of the buildings on the streets.
So I fought back.
They dragged me into the car
And soon broke my teeth on every landing
Of a six-floor walk-up.

In a zoo-stop room piled with beer cans,
I was thrown down onto the bed.
A dim light shone from the corner
Where a humpty-dumpty radio blared from a
Radiator.

O go ahead, hit me.
Hit me!

You men of THE LAW.
Someday, this country will
Practice JUSTICE...
Come on! HIT ME.
Spit at me. REACH OUT!
O, what's a girl to do.
Put It in my mouth,
If you must,
Officers... Sweet trip to PARADISE.

Playing a sadistic game, each brute razored,
Razored me under the ribs.
Like perfect butchers, they cut
    And they cut me:
        This one is for your mammy.
        This one is for King.
        This one is for your FUCKIN' PEOPLE.
        This one is for You too,
            Freak queen nigger bitch.

Then,
They stopped slashing me.
It was decided that I shouldn't
    Be killed —
        A STAY OF EXECUTION.

One of the BRUTES wanted to fuck me
My arm went numb.
The bullet moved
And I messed on myself, choking back the tears.

The other men cheered, drank beer
And kept joking
As their fellow THORN pumped his big cock
In my pudding.
And can you believe it,
All I could think about
Was THE BULLET IN BLUE'S HEAD.

Madness engulfed me.
I reached for the man's balls.
I PULLED. One was in my hands.
Somehow, I made it to the doorway.
I made it to the street,
Running...
RUNning...
RUNNING.
Tears overwhelming,
No one would help me.
Blood gushing from my ass,
Blood in the streets,
Blood all over me,
Naked...
One Rawdog Night
When TOO MUCH of my Queer
Was SHOWING,
I let out such a howl.

>   Death moved heavy
>   Like storms and torrent
>   And not much different
>   Than our adjustable assortment
>   Of harsh lies:

Like NIGGERS should go crazy
Rather than UNIFY.

Yes, the radiant soul depths
Of our struggling black seeds
Fall apart
As we hate each other dearly,
Only to criticize unduly.
YES, WE CRITICIZE AND BLEED.
Never to realize
That special sharing space Where our spirits
Can behold the Universe
And rise.
FIRE NEXT TIME.

PHILL WILSON

WHEN YOUR LOVER HAS AIDS

It is the breaking of your heart every time you have to leave him in the hospital. It is having to leave him in the hospital, too often. It is being a member of the team that makes the decisions about his care. It is making the final decisions all by yourself.

It is the echoing of his voice in your head on the eve of his death when he says to you, "Take me home!" It is the echo of your voice in the hollow of your heart created by the pain.

It is feeling the pain and knowing each bit of hurt is a celebration of the love you feel for each other. It is the chuckle in his voice when he awakes from the coma in the middle of the night to tell you he loves you. It is telling him you love him as he takes his last breath. It is telling him it's OK. It is telling him you'll be OK.

It is holding him and feeling the warmness of life leave his body.

It is weird, so very, very weird. It is probably the weirdest thing you'll ever experience.

It is believing that if you work hard enough, fast enough, long enough, if you can keep him on the cutting edge of treatment, maybe he won't die. It is the anger when he dies anyway. It is the guilt because maybe you didn't work hard enough, fast enough or long enough. It is the hopelessness of knowing even a love as great as yours could not save his life.

154

It is saying: "I'm fine. I'll take care of everything. I'll handle it." It is discovering that you are not fine. You can't take care of anything, and this time you can't handle it.

It is feeling cheated because it was supposed to be forever and it was only for ten years.

It is remembering in the middle of the day and feeling as if it were happening all over again. It is the loneliness, because you have no other friend like him.

It is calling your landlord to find out how much the rent is or calling the bank to find out what your balance is because he did those things.

It is sitting at home and wondering what's keeping him because you forgot he's not coming home. It is keeping the tape on the answering machine because it is a way of hearing his voice.

It is being glad to return home after a trip because you know the cats miss him nearly as much as you do. It is keeping his driver's license, wearing both of your wedding bands, and isolating yourself from family and friends because you don't know what else to do.

It is wishing he were here. It is knowing that he is.

It is driving down the freeway and being blinded by your tears. It is not knowing that you are crying.

It is wondering what will happen to you when your time comes, and he is not there to send you home. It is knowing he will be there.

It is the numbness, the panic, the fear, the sadness. It is the blind rage over what's happening to you.

It is not chronic. It is not manageable. It is not over. Even after he dies.

RICHARD WITHERSPOON

HAIKU

straight as bamboo
identical twins differ
peeling eggplant

DONALD WOODS

WE BE YOUNG

For Maxavier

we take turns
with the steam iron
the julep face mask
the eyeliner

we young
taking turns
in the mirror
on the phone

we fine
spend the day
dreaming of the night
spiky punch
the white balloons
grown men gyrate
beautiful girls
tipsy in polka dots

we at the door
they check for weapons
yank lucky keith
from our caravan
to flirt and

we shimmy
disguise our tremors
fear delight
diagonal crossing
in an imaginary spotlight
beg the ganja gods
for equilibrium
perfect balance

in platform shoes
we made it
the staircase
rickety and wide
cloudy crowded
the hat-wearing crew sneers
the conga mobilizes pointy limbs
sends them pushing
through human foliage

we movin'
makin' up shit
max in sunglasses trippin'
fling our heads like we got hair
hunch our shoulders 'round our ears

we steal looks
at his highness of harlem
his majesty dark
knight of the subway

we use our hands
as spanish lady fans
he is night into morning
intimate of the big bopper
friend of the limo drivers

we bold now and
he winks
we titter and
he lumbers
sprawls among
a thousand dancing feet

vibrates to his own music

we scream
ladies-in-waiting gasp
and he is erectus
coated with the lofty dust
we wait
he reclines in dark corners
cushions grimy with sweat
tokes a joint
beckons to the crowd

the supplicant
wiry with shiny limbs
collapses at the knees
folds at the waist
pours into his waiting arms

we crushed
hiss hiss hiss
and snap snap besides
we shuffle
to the men's room
soggy with toilet paper
walls and floors
stare at ourselves
in a tiny mirror
take turns
staring at the promise
in our eyes

we fine
we fine we

know we fine
dressed in white
smiling bright
try again and

we try again
to manage a ballroom of
faces masked in hallucination
contorted by their own beauty
features stacked against recognition
valiant we
dive into the tweeters
shove our butts against
the big ones
the black throbbing speakers
toss us about

we insistent clouds
grayed by sticky sweat and
love whispers
through bended knees

we brave
shoulder-to-shoulder sissies
on the crest of manhood
twirling like tomorrow
is certain
dipping and diving
like the future
like forever

we fine
we know we fine

looking tomorrow
in the gold tooth
the hazy early sunlight
taking turns
kissing and hugging
adieu

we fine
on the crest of something
twirling and spinning
the future
hugging then
kissing
adieu

WRATH

DISCIPLINE

Inside my hand
a leather strap
50 times
across your back
just to see if your screams
are as obnoxious as your speech
to see if they hold more wisdom
than your words

Shackled to the bedpost
straining against your bonds
just to see if you're so arrogant
in fear
just to see if you're so beautiful
in pain

Between my teeth a razor blade
your beauty soon to be unmade
Just to see if you can writhe
as sexy as you dance
to see if your grimace is
as phony as your smile

Invaded by a leather phallus
crying in humiliation
degraded by deliberate malice
intent upon your subjugation
just to see if you're so arrogant
in fear
just to see if you're so beautiful
in pain
to show you that the world is not your friend
to prove to you that this is not a game

ALLEN WRIGHT

m.

he lipped a trumpet
like he kissed
a man   without
pressure

BIL WRIGHT

MIRACLE

If time holds a miracle
we'll dance together
as two old men:
sunstroke scalps
dropped buttocks, watery thighs.
But our hands
how our bony, veiny, trembling hands
will find their partners
palm to palm, fingers rung round each other
and hold on tight
tight.
Dance me
dance me across the floor.
I'll stay with you
if time holds a miracle.

GARY PAUL WRIGHT

THE HEATHEN

Visiting home one Christmastime
Sitting with old friends
Chitchatting on 'bout this n' that
The odds and all the ends
We talked a lot 'bout love n' stuff
The ups and then the downs
When one friend noticed my ample grin
Had turned into a major frown.

"What's wrong with you?" he questioned me
"Why is your face so long?
In all this talk 'bout finding love
Did we say something wrong?"
"No, it's not that," I told him flatly
"It's not just what you've said
But this talk of love confuses me
It's cloggin' up my head!

"See, I want love for love itself
And I must say I am tryin'
But love and sex go hand in hand
That too must be satisfyin'
The men I've had were well and good
But something seems to be missin'
Don't know what it is, but there must be more
Than simply huggin' n' kissin'."

My friend just smiled then took my hand
And said as he looked into my eyes
"I have an answer for you
But it ain't no big surprise
You need somebody who keeps you sweatin'
Instead of simply breathin'
It ain't just a man you gotta git
Child, git yourself a HEATHEN!"

"A HEATHEN?" I asked with true concern
"Just what the hell is that?
You mean I have to find a guy
Who walks 'round with a bat?"
"Oh, no, my dear," he answered me
"Tho' you're not far from the truth
'Cause it's what he got between his legs
That signifies this brute.

"A HEATHEN is one with a big ol' thang
And he knows just how to use it
Once you git the feel of it
Baby, you can't refuse it
He usually has these great big lips
The kind that devours
But as soon as you git a taste
You'll be smackin' them thangs for hours!"

I sat there astounded and could not believe
What was coming out of his mouth
But some little devil inside my head
Knew just what he was talkin' 'bout
I cleared my throat and then I said
"Well, guess I must be leavin'
But before I go, please tell me more
'Bout this thing you call a HEATHEN."

"He's generally large," my friend informed
"Good-lookin', Black and bold
Muscles bulgin' all over the place
A beauty to behold
Tho' not too bright, I must admit
His instincts are extreme
And when it comes to makin' love
This man will make you scream!

"He starts out kinda rough, you know
Just to show you who's the boss
And if you're a virgin to these proceedings
You won't regret the loss
He means no harm nor violent acts
So you don't have to fret
But if you've offered him your stuff
Your stuff he's gonna get!

"His giant hands help you relax
He soothes you with his laughter
But not for a moment does he let you forget
He knows just what he's after
When you are primed, he positions you
And lifts you oh so gently
Body poised and arrow aimed
He slowly makes his entry.

"You try to squirm, you gasp for breath
The initial pain's frightenin'
But he persists his forward thrust
And soon your pleasure's heightenin'
As bodies adjust to become one
A rhythm starts and grows
Then you feel his manhood swell
From your head down to your toes.

"Once inside, he stops for a while
So you git used to the feelin'
You find yourself a-beggin' him
To git your head a-reelin'
Obligin' you the motion starts
He grabs for a better stance
The ins and outs increase a bit
Your body then begins its dance.

"His forward punch inspires you
Your backside moves in perfect time
You rock and roll each other 'til
Both bodies and spirits rhyme
Just when it seems you can't take more
Of this locomotive boon
His built-up energy explodes
And causes you to croon and swoon.

"As he collapses on top of you
His exercise well-spent
You heave a sigh of grand relief
'Cause this was heaven-sent
So listen child, before you go
Life sometimes is uneven
But git off your high horse
And git yourself a HEATHEN!"

I thanked my friend most graciously
For sharing this advice
Knowing damn sure his well-formed words
I'd consider at least twice
And heading home, the little devil
That was playing with my mind
Told me a HEATHEN was what I needed
And a HEATHEN I'd better find.

Six months later I find myself
Laying in your mighty arms
Full of joy and much in love
With more than just your charms
'Cause you have got the perfect sense
To know what turns me on
And when you push those buttons, man
To fantasyland I am gone.

Now as you sleep, I thank the Lord
For sending you my way
And I thank my friend of Christmastime
Each and every single day
'Cause it was his words that set me right
As surely as I am breathin'
The best advice I ever got
Was "GIT YOURSELF A HEATHEN!"

CONTRIBUTORS

Lawrence Dewyatt Abrams is a recent graduate of Yale University. His creative work has appeared in *Black/Out* and *Ritual & Dissent.* Currently, he is completing work on *A Storm's Passing*, his first novel.

Oye Apeji Ajanaku was born in Memphis, Tennessee, on August 27, 1942. His family moved in 1947 to Chicago, Illinois, where he grew up on the Southside. At seventeen, he dropped out of school and joined the navy and served for four years. He returned to Memphis in 1963, "looking for roots," and has made it his ever since. He is openly gay and has been publicly active in the struggle for gay rights for a number of years. He was a contributor to Joseph Beam's *In the Life*, and his poetry has appeared in the journal of Black and White Men Together.

Akhenaton is thirty years old, currently lives in New York City. Previously unpublished, he writes haiku, tanka and short stories.

Sabah As-Sabah was born on May 3, 1966, in New York City. Sabah has attended both New York University and the University of Massachusetts at Amherst. He now resides at The New School for Social Research where he is completing his major in writing and literature. "I feel that the bridge that has to be crossed between the perils of separation can only be done within the boundaries of solidarity. My interest in my sisters and brothers does not stop at sexual orientation. Neither are my alliances so superficial. My only interest is effecting a change, to bring this galling infrastructure to a final, all-encompassing collapse."

Thom Bean resides in San Francisco. Bean currently publishes *Quarterly Interchange,* a magazine for men interested in interracial and cross-cultural relationships. Bean also published *The Castro Express.* Bean has been published in the *Advocate, Out/Look, Windy City Times, Bay Times.* Bean contributed to the anthology *Black Men/White Men.* A long-time activist, Bean is a founding member and first president of Black and White Men Together-San Francisco Bay Area. Bean has served as a director on the *Out/Look* Foundation Board, was co-chair of "The Coalition for Human Rights" with Carole Migden, co-founded "Racism and Homophobia in the Media" with Pat Norman. Bean currently serves on the Gay and Lesbian Alliance Against Defamation-San Francisco Bay Area Board, GLAAD/USA National Steering Committee and as a national director of the National Association of Black and White Men Together.

Blackberri is a performer who was born on May 31, 1945. He may be the most visible African-American gay man. A singer and songwriter, he began his career with the Gunther Quint Band, later forming two bands: Breeze in 1973 and Blackberri and Friends in 1979. He appeared in the 1977 gay film *Word Is Out*, which featured his song, "It's Okay." He has recorded two albums, *Walls to Roses* and *Finally*. His song "Eat the Rich" won the Songwriters Resource and Services songwriting contest. His music is heard in the film *Looking for Langston*, and he appears in the film *Tongues Untied*.

Eric Stephen Booth was born and raised in Oceanhill-Brownsville, Brooklyn, New York. A graduate of CCNY, three of his plays have been produced — including *Metamorphosis (A Slice of Black Gay Life)*. He has had various poems and short stories published in gay and straight magazines. Eric's ambition is to write about the deep dark feelings that we lock up in our memory banks.

Bernard Branner (born 1/22/57) directs Flesh and Spirit, a collaborative performance company. He teaches Haitian dance in San Francisco. His publications include *Clay Drum, In the Life, Five Fingers Review* and his first collected works entitled *Red Bandanas* (scheduled for fall release). He co-authored and performs *Fierce Love: Stories of Black Gay Life* along with Brian Freeman and Eric Gupton. He appeared in Marlon Riggs' films *Tongues Untied* and *Anthem*. He holds an M.A. in Interdisciplinary Arts.

Rory Buchanan is thirty-five, and he lives in Brooklyn, New York, with his seventeen-year-old son. His work has appeared in *The Pyramid Periodical* and been anthologized in *Brother to Brother*. He is an educator with the Minority Task Force on AIDS in New York City.

John E. Bush was born in Wellsville, Ohio, on December 8, 1927. He was educated in the Wellsville public schools and graduated from Delaware State College with a B.A. He received an M.S.Ed. from Westminster College, New Wilmington, Pennsylvania, and an M.A. and Ph.D in Sociology from the University of Pittsburgh. He has been very active in the National Association of Black and White Men Together (served as co-chair and treasurer, and currently edits the *National Newsletter*). He is professor of sociology at Southeastern Massachusetts University.

Chuck Butler was born on 10/17/54 and hails from Atlantic City. Recently his first play *The Third Rhythm* was produced for a limited engagement at the world-famous Apollo Theatre and is now slated for off-Broadway. His choreopoem *Blackmale: Admissible Evidence* is also slated for the stage. Currently Chuck is directing Hazelle Goodman's *An Evening with Hazelle*, a one-woman show, and he is writing the book for a musical to star Johnny Kemp.

Rickey Butler was born in St. Louis, Missouri. He's twenty-three years

173

old, and this is his first published work.

Bland J. "BJ" Carr began writing in his last year at City College of New York. His work has appeared in *Black/Out, Class and Reflections: The Journal of the U.N. Society of Writers.*

Don Charles

Birthdate: June 24, 1960
Birthplace: Kansas City, Missouri
Hair: red
Eyes: brown
Complexion: bronze
Politics: progressive
Sexual preference: reciprocal men of color
Best friend: God
Favorite music: disco & 60's pop/rock
Favorite color: red
Likes: for-real people
Hates: bullshit people, war, chit'lins, conservatism.

J. Coleman is a native of Washington, D.C. He was born in 1953. He was educated in the D.C. public schools and in two private universities. He holds degrees in linguistics and a foreign language. Mr. Coleman hopes his piano playing will continue to improve his poetry, and that his poetry will continue to improve his piano playing. His poetry has appeared in the newsletter of the D.C. Chapter of Black and White Men Together. Mr. Coleman's first "poetic inspiration" was his maternal grandmother, herself a poet and songwriter.

Carl Cook was born on December 5, 1950, in Philadelphia, the City of Brotherly Love; poetry and painting were preoccupations since childhood, conduits to a world full of good and evil, a challenge to transcend; now at forty, an educator of the very young and still looking for true love, if such things exist.

André De Shields is the Distinguished Visiting Professor in the theatre division of the Meadows School of the Arts at Southern Methodist University in Dallas, Texas. Mr. De Shields achieved national acclaim for creating the title role in the Broadway musical *The Wiz* and for his Emmy Award-winning performance in the NBC television special *Ain't Misbehavin'*. He is the creator of *Saint Tous*: a music-theatre piece based on the life and times of Toussaint L'Ouverture. 'Nuff said.

Rodney Dildy was born on July 23, 1953. He is a BGM living and working in NYC. One of the founding board members of Other Countries, he is also the president of Kafra Publishing Co. and publisher/editor of *The Pyramid Periodical: The Provocative Journal of Black Gay Folk*. He has been seropositive for about three years.

174

Melvin Dixon is the author of two novels: *Vanishing Rooms* (Dutton,1991) and *Trouble the Water* (University of Colorado, 1989). His recent poems appear in the *Kenyon Review* and *The James White Review* and recent fiction in the anthology *Breaking Ice* edited by Terry McMillan (Penguin, 1990).

Sean Drakes, a native of Trinidad & Tobago, is a budding freelance artist/documentarian creating from Brooklyn.

Errol A. Edwards was born thirty-six years ago in Aruba, Netherlands Antilles. "I have been writing since my teens. My writings are drawn from life experiences, dreams and the realities of being a black gay man, HIV+, a Queer Nation activist, a New York City Gay Men's Chorus tenor, a romantic who is blessed with guardian-angel friends."

Troynell Edwards is a writer living in New York City.

Abba Elethea (James W. Thompson) conducts a poetry workshop at the Frederick Douglass Arts Center, New York City. His choreopoems *Songs for My Sisters* and *Eye Ellipse/Ear Eternal: Soul So Sweet* premiered at La MaMa E.T.C. His poems and short stories have appeared in numerous anthologies and periodicals: *Black Poetry of the 20th Century, Blackspirits, Black Poets, You Better Believe It, Obsidian, Black World, TransAtlantic Review, Antioch Review* and *Présence Africaine* among others. His books are *First Fire, The Antioch Suite Jazz* and the forthcoming *Songs for my Sisters* and *Poems Old and New*.

Larry Ferguson is a poet presenting images that are often disturbing, thought-provoking and challenging. The work draws from Ferguson's fifteen-year involvement in national and local struggles for social justice and the individual struggle of coming to grips with one's reality.

Salih Michael Fisher was born in Harlem in 1956. He is an active member of Men of All Colors Together/New York. His poems have appeared in the anthologies *Black Men/White Men, Gay & Lesbian Poetry in Our Time* and *Other Countries*.

Guy-Mark Foster was born in Logan, West Virginia, in 1959. His work has appeared in *The Pyramid Periodical, The James White Review* and in the anthologies *Shadows of Love* and *Brother to Brother*. He currently lives in New York City.

David Warren Frechette was a prominent journalist who died on May 11, 1991, of AIDS-related complications. His essays, reviews and interviews appeared in *The City Sun, Penthouse, New York Native*, the *Advocate, Essence, The Amsterdam News, Black Film Review* and *Gentlemen's Quarterly*. His poems and short stories have been published in *RFD*, *In Your Face*, *The Pyramid Periodical*, *Out/Look* and the anthology *Brother to Brother*. He was actively involved in the organizations Men of All Colors Together/New York, Gay Men of African Descent, Gay Males S/M Activists and Other Countries. David loved good food (remember his own glorious pecan pies, quiches and meat loafs?), good films, good theater, good music, good sex (remember the scandalous pictures that accompanied the tales of sexual escapades?): *the good life*.

Thomas Glave, was born and raised in the Bronx, New York. He has published poetry in *Pulpsmith*, *The Midwest Poetry Review*, *Cottonwood* and other magazines. Currently a student majoring in Latin American Studies and English at Bowdoin College, he divides his time between writing and working in Oakland, California, and Brunswick, Maine.

Roy Gonsalves, "I'm not telling my age or birthday, so forget it. I'm young, beautiful, Black and gay." In addition to being a writer, Roy Gonsalves is a visual artist, therapist and performing artist. His work has appeared in *Essence*, *Other Countries*, *Bay Windows*, *The Pyramid Periodical* and in his newly released book *Perversion*, which was nominated for a 1991 Gregory Kolovakos Award for AIDS Writing.

Kenton Michael Grey — age thirty-two, was born and raised in the Midwest. He now resides in New York City. An original member of the Other Countries Writing Workshop, his energies are now divided between his work as a computer consultant, his writing, his clothing design and filmmaking.

Mark A. Haile was born on November 17, 1956, in the Mediterranean city of Tarabulus, Libya. His birthsite has been destroyed by American bombing. A journalist for *BLK* and co-editor of *Kuumba*, he also writes poetry, fiction, and lyrics. He lives in the Chinatown district of Los Angeles.

Craig G. Harris is a thirtysomething-year-old Afrofemcentric griot whose work has appeared in *In the Life* (Alyson), *Gay Life* (Dolphin/Doubleday), *New Men, New Minds* (Crossing Press), and *Brother to Brother* (Alyson). He is constantly seeking creative solutions to the HIV pandemic.

Keith M. Harris is a twenty-six-year-old gay Afro-American. "I was born and raised in Wilson, North Carolina. Presently, I am living and working in Oakland, California."

Lyle Ashton Harris graduated from Wesleyan University in 1987 and recently completed a masters degree in fine arts from the California Institute of the Arts in Los Angeles. He was raised in the Bronx, New York, and he has lived and traveled in Africa and Northern Europe. His photographs have been exhibited throughout the United States and England. Reviews and articles on Harris' work have appeared in *Newstatesman Society, Afterimage, Mother Jones, Artweek, TEN-8, Out/Look* and the *San Francisco Examiner.* Harris' monumental black-and-white self-portraits titled "Reclaiming Sensuality '88" were on exhibit at the Contemporary Arts Center in New Orleans, Louisiana, through April 1991.

Reginald Harris is an Associate Librarian for Baltimore, Maryland's Enoch Pratt Library. He is a founding member of BUGLE (Blacks United for Gay and Lesbian Equality) and sits on the administrative committee of the William Wolfe Institute for Gay and Lesbian Studies. Reggie's work has previously appeared in *Black/Out*.

L. D. Hartfield-Coe was born in Seguin, Texas, in the fifties. His poetry has appeared in *Blackheart, RFD, Seattle Gay News* and various college literary journals. Unpublished works include some twelve manuscripts. His current work in progress is entitled Lovejoy: A Manuscript of Visionary Love. He resides in Seattle, Washington.

Jeff A. Haskins writes in an Afrocentric voice that is rooted in both his spirituality and sexuality. His rich legacy hails from West Africa to the plantations of Georgia, to the Freedman's Hospital on the Howard University campus where he was born and graduated. After receiving his M.F.A. in Theatre Management, he worked for major theatres in the New York area. He is presently the general manager of Rainbow Repertory Theatre. After testing for HIV, Jeff became involved as an advocate for the African holistic approach to medicine and has been successful at using this method to save his own life. Jeff has finally come out this year as a poet, performer and director. He made his directorial debut with Reginald T. Jackson's play *Sixty-Nine*, which has been presented throughout New York City. Jeff makes his publishing debut in this anthology. He is a Taurus with a Capricorn rising. He was born on 5/14/55, a number 5 person, four times over.

Essex Hemphill is the editor of *Brother to Brother: New Writings by Black Gay Men.*

B.Michael Hunter, a.k.a. Bert Hunter, mama's third child, loves and is inspired by written words. He works to share them with the world. "Don't want no doors left unopened, and I ain't about to leave things like they are!"

F. Spencer Irvin was born on June 5, 1966, and recently decided to pursue his writing career. Most of his recent works deal with common daily emotions of African-American gay men as well as brazen sexual topics of men on men. As a poet, he wants to write what most of us want to say but don't.

Isaac Jackson is a writer whose work spans many genres. His poetry has been anthologized twice by Gay Men's Press of London (*Tongues Untied: Five Black Gay Male Poets* and *Not Love Alone: A Modern Gay Anthology*), and has appeared as well in numerous gay publications. A short story appears in *The Gay Nineties*, an anthology of fiction published by *The James White Review* and Crossing Press. *Somebody's New Pajamas*, a picture book for children, is in press with Dial Books for Young Readers.

G. Winston James was born on December 11, 1967, in Kingston, Jamaica, and moved to Paterson, New Jersey, at the age of three. He received several literary awards in high school, including the William Carlos Williams prize upon his graduation in 1985. While a student at Columbia University, he served as editor of the school's *Black Heights* literary magazine. He is currently working towards the publication of his first poetry collection.

Redvers JeanMarie was an actor and writer who died of AIDS-related complications on February 15, 1989. He appeared on the stage in *King Lear* with the New York Shakespeare Festival and in Peter Nichol's *National Health* in Paris. He was the nonfiction editor of *Other Countries*. He served on the national board of Black and White Men Together.

Richard E. Jennings: "I was born on 11/14/58 and am the youngest of three. Some of my interests include movies, music and reading. I have been writing poetry for about seven years. I am a 1988 graduate from Huston-Tillotson College."

Samuel Augustus Jennings was born on December 4, 1944, and migrated to Maryland from Florida several years ago. His compositions have appeared in *AMTRAK News*, *Passenger Train Journal*, *The Pyramid Periodical* and *National Railway Bulletin*. He performs with the Baltimore-based Actors Against Drugs (AAD): a theater troupe spotlighting alcohol and drug addiction and the AIDS crisis. Sam works aboard AMTRAK trains. Between trips he is a volunteer with PROJECT 2000, which is a Black mentoring program for African-American primary school boys. "Hi-Speed Queen" is dedicated to his daughter Erika.

Brad Johnson is a graduate of Yale University (1974) whose work has been published in *Essence*, *The Pyramid Periodical*, *In the Life* (Alyson), *Other Countries* and the *Nassau Gator Gazette*, a newspaper printed on board the USS Nassau (LHA-4), upon which he served in the U.S. Navy.

Cary Alan Johnson is an author, activist, and Africanist from New York City.

Sidney Curtis Johnson is twenty-five. He was born and raised in Camden County, New Jersey. Sidney has studied dance and journalism in Philadelphia. He has danced in the Philadelphia/New York area for the past ten years. Sidney is also an experienced choreographer. This is the first publication in which Sidney's work will reach a national audience that he plans to reach with more works.

K. Maurice Jones: the writings of k. maurice jones encompass the black male sensibility — with self-definition as the prevailing theme. dub / jazz / hi-life / reggae / r&b / gospel / blues / new jack swing / rap / dreadlocks / conks / crewcuts / fades / the dozens / sermons / fathers / deacons / sugarmen / lovers / nephews / acebooncoons / all git buck wild in his poetry, essays and articles.

Anthony B. Knight-Dewey was born and raised in Queens, New York. In addition to being a writer, he is a translator and Cultural Affairs Consultant of the African Diaspora. His strong desire to explore his own African-Latin roots took him to Venezuela where he lived for many years. He now makes his home in Washington, D.C., where he is presently working on a project with the Smithsonian Institution and completing a Masters/Ph.D. program in sociolinguistics at Georgetown.

Steve Langley, a singer-songwriter and poet, can be seen in the award-winning film *Tongues Untied*. His poetry has appeared in *Other Countries*, *Black/Out* and other publications. One of his musical compositions, "In This Land," has been performed by the internationally acclaimed a cappella group Sweet Honey in the Rock.

Cedric Levon (born August 3, 1967) is a native of Winston-Salem, North Carolina. He now resides in San Francisco. He received degrees from the University of North Carolina at Chapel Hill and Stanford University. This is his first published piece. He ultimately seeks BGM solidarity and empowerment.

Joseph Long, a.k.a. Acebi Mtubeebi, was born on March 3, 1938, in Harlem, New York. A self-proclaimed griot, community health educator and public speaker on Living Without Alcohol and Drugs While Living with HIV Illness and AIDS in African Communities. A registered nurse, he holds a B.S. in Nursing and Urban Culture from Wayne County and Touro College. He also holds an M.S. in Adult Education and Human Resource Development. Publications: *PWA Coalition Newsline*, *Griot NY*, *Vancouver Press*, *Phoenix Wildfire*. Long is also a member of the Other Countries collective.

Harvey J. Lucas was born in Baltimore, Maryland, in May of 1962. Spent six years in the United States Air Force; continental U.S. and abroad. Now living in Washington, D.C., he currently studies at the District of Columbia University. Three works published in the fall of

1989 edition of *The Pyramid Periodical*. Recording life uncensored. *Penda wewe rafiki zangu.* (Swahili for "Love you, my friends.")

Jerome Mack, a native of Holly Hill, South Carolina, is a former New York City bus operator who now works as a supervisor at a shelter for homeless men. He began enhancing his writing abilities a few years ago, after living with his significant brother who gave much encouragement and confidence. He has been published in *The Pyramid Periodical*.

Scott Mackey is a native of Texas. He currently lives and works in New York City.

Vernon Maulsby: born on 1/30/57, in a small town in upstate New York. "I knew that I was gay early on but fought it until my twenties. Began writing in 1985, first poem in 1986. My work has appeared in *Fag Rag*, *Phila Poets*, *Gay Community News*, *Black Masks*, *Black/Out*, *Short Fuse* and other lit mags."

Rodney McCoy, Jr., is a poet born and bred in Brooklyn, New York, where he currently resides. Born on August 27, 1967, he received his B.A. from Oberlin College in 1989, and he now works for the Minority Task Force on AIDS as a health educator. This is his first published work, and he hopes many more will follow.

Bob McNeil: "I was born in St. Vincent, the Virgin Islands, in 1965, and educated in America. I, the student scribe, am pursuing higher education; majoring in experiential philosophy and word alchemy. My poems are as varied as the publications they've appeared in. 'Serving Man' is from a manuscript entitled *Secular Sacraments*."

Metaphora is a young New York City-based poet and musician. He has read his work at Playwrights Horizon Theater, the West End Cafe and the Nuyorican Poet's Cafe. Part of his mission as a poet is to exalt the black queens of the diaspora — for they are, indeed, cultural griots.

Alan E. Miller writes: "I am an 'out' high school English teacher who resides in Oakland, CA. My poems have appeared in *GCN*, *Out/Look*, *Brother to Brother* and in my chapbook *at the club*. You can see my face in Marlon Riggs' video *Tongues Untied*.

Jim Murell crash landed. This world. Somewhere near Toronto, March 11, 1952. Sole survivor. Strange child. Raised in the Bronx by Gladys and Jim. Raised in loving sacrifice. Raised in the music and nurturing of Capote, Baldwin, Morrison, Walcott, Young, Rukeyser, Wilde and Neruda. Healers, shamans, griots of earth's tribe.

John S. Patterson (1936-   ) "I am a black, gay, progressive, sane, sober, working-class man in a world that tends to be otherwise. Born in Montour Falls, New York, I grew up in the 'inner city' of Syracuse, which we just called 'home.' I attended the public schools and spent most of my time being president of things, gaining most of my early education by imitating the reading habits of my father, Jessie, also a poet. After graduation from Colgate and Ohio universities, I spent two years in the U.S. Army and three years in the civil rights movement. For the past nine years I have travelled the country performing solo shows based on my life and on poetry by black Americans. My most recent performance was as candidate for Congress on the New Alliance Party line.

Reginald Patterson was involved with Other Countries. He died in New York City of AIDS-related complications in December 1988.

Robert E. Penn was born on March 19, 1948. "If I die young, don't you dare get in a pulpit and lament my gifted, assimilated self succumbing to intravenous drug use. 'Cause I never touched a needle, nor got a transfusion. I'm not hemophiliac, nor was I born of an HIV-positive mama. If I die before an African-American man's usual paltry sixty years, it'll be an accident or, more likely, from HIV received while making love, as best I knew how, to another man. Amen."

Eleo Pomare is the artistic director and choreographer of the Eleo Pomare Dance Company. Mr. Pomare was born in Colombia, South America. His company has challenged the sensitivities of sophisticated dance audiences at Broadway's ANTA Theatre, Washington's John F. Kennedy Center for the Performing Arts, New York's City Center and Joyce Theater, Montreal's Theatre Maisonneuve, and the Adelaide Festival of Arts in Australia; and it has toured throughout the United States, Canada, Puerto Rico, the West Indies, Australia, Italy, Germany, Holland, Sweden and Norway. In addition to maintaining his own company, Mr. Pomare has choreographed works for the Alvin Ailey Dance Company, the Maryland Ballet Company, the Dayton Contemporary Dance Company, the Cleo Parker-Robinson Dance Company (Denver), Alpha and Omega Dance Company, the National Ballet of Holland, Balletinstituttet (Oslo, Norway), the Australian Contemporary Dance Company and the Ballet Palacio das Artes (Belo Horizonte, Brazil). In addition to the John Jay Whitney Fellowship, Mr. Pomare is a Guggenheim Fellow and he has been awarded National Endowment for the Arts choreographer's grants in 1975, 1982, 1988 and 1989.

Charles R. P. Pouncy was born in South Carolina on June 4, 1954. He is a graduate of Fordham University and the Cornell Law School. His work appears in *Other Countries* and *Brother to Brother*. His play *Kids* was produced in 1989 by the Rainbow Repertory Theatre Company based in New York City.

Craig A. Reynolds was born in Washington, D.C., on September 14, 1952. He has remained in the area to obtain his formal education and to pursue his career. Craig has taught on the college level, was a publications manager at the World Bank, and he is a writer-editor at the Smithsonian Institution.

L. Phillip Richardson (12/24/49) is a native New Yorker and for the last five years an intense Brazilophile, forever encouraged by the continuity of African traditions across the diaspora — at home and abroad. He has published his first short story "On the Line" in *Other Countries*. He is pleased to make his poetic debut here.

Colin Robinson, a Trinidadian immigrant, is trying to become better known as ... (pronounced el-lip-sis, and always spelled with three periods — never four). ... has assumed the strategic identity of a black gay man living in Brooklyn, and is trying, through writing, activism, crossdressing and group process, to figure out who ... is. An artist and an administrator with Other Countries, ... works at a Bronx AIDS service organization. ...'s lips and work appear in Marlon Riggs' new short video *Anthem*.

Harold McNeil Robinson was born on August 7, 1948, and attended Phillips Academy in Andover, Massachusetts, Saint Olaf College in Northfield, Minnesota, and San Francisco State University. He returned to his place of birth, Brooklyn, New York, in 1983, after teaching and training in Minnesota, California, Saudi Arabia and North Yemen. He is a past president of Gay Men of African Descent and a practicing massage therapist. His work has appeared in *The Pyramid Periodical*, *B&G Magazine* and *The Journal of the National Association of Black and White Men Together*.

Philip Robinson, forty years old, a native New Yorker, migrated to Boston some twenty-one years ago to pursue his education at Emerson College. Philip writes about being gay, black and male, so as not to create even a shadow of doubt as to who he is. "Never diminish yourself through misrepresentation." His first book of poems, *Secret Passages: A Trilogy of Thought* (Vantage Press), was published in 1987. He is the recipient of The Audre Lorde Award for Poetry, presented by the Greater Boston Lesbian/Gay Political Alliance. He is the Student Service Coordinator and AIDS Coordinator at the Grover Cleveland Middle School in Boston. He and his companion of ten years, Joseph Jackson, live in Jamaica Plain, Massachusetts.

Assoto Saint was born in Haiti and lives in New York City. He is outspoken on his HIV-positive status. He was awarded a 1990 Fellowship in Poetry from the New York Foundation for the Arts. He was the recipient of the 1990 James Baldwin Award from the Black Gay

& Lesbian Leadership Forum.

Bryan Scott was born in London, England, and came to America in 1970. He first started writing essays and poetry while studying Speech & Language Pathology at Hampton Institute, of which he is a graduate. Mr. Scott has had some work published and received recognition in the "World of Poetry." He is an accomplished makeup artist and actor, and he teaches dance to preteens in his community. Bryan feels that there's always a new experience to write about because life is constantly changing. Therefore, as writers and poets, we must share our pain, which then allows us to fortify our spirit.

Carlos Segura was born in the Dominican Republic and raised in New York City. His work has appeared in *The Pyramid Periodical*. Carlos works as a health educator for the Minority Task Force on AIDS in New York City.

Gabriel Sims is a transplanted Louisianan living in Dallas whose hobbies include working out, running and reading. "I'm a black man who wears cowboy boots. I'm in the Reserves. I'm also a Christian who believes that God has a purpose for me being here, and that all things work together for good."

Neil Sims was born in 1951, the same year as his friend Bart Gorin who died on Valentine's Day, 1991. "Bushmaster" is a curse. "I send it to all the profiteers of misery who wait to let things die, who suck my world grey. I love you, Bart."

Jamez L. Smith was born December 2, 1963. "I have lived in Montgomery, Newark, San Francisco, Los Angeles, Vancouver, British Columbia, & Brighton, England. I presently live in Seattle. I spent four years in the USAF as Flight Simulator Technician. I still work at simulation. Jesus Christ is most important in my life."

Sur Rodney (Sur), resident alien, born in Montreal, takes his name from Surrealism. Published a book of his poems in 1981. Performed with the Blackheart Collective in the "early years." Recognized for his involvement with the contemporary visual arts and photography. Lives and works in N.Y.C., Paris, and London.

Rodger Taylor was born on November 23, 1952. Rodger currently lives in Dayton, Ohio, where he was raised. He is committed to his involvement as a therapist in a treatment program that focuses on the challenge of "high-risk" adolescents. As a classical pianist, Rodger also performs in the Dayton area and teaches privately.

Terence Taylor is a devoted scriptwriter/graphic artist living in Los Angeles. He believes in the Tao, reincarnation, the redemptive power of music and the honesty of children. He will never grow up, though he hopes to mature, and often refers to himself in the third person.

Duncan E. Teague: "Looking back, I remember writing comedy in the eighth grade at Emmanuel Lutheran Grade School in Kansas City where I grew up. Later, I learned to express my feelings in countless letters to pen pals during high school. Those letters were my first poems. After coming out to Reverend and Mrs. Teague in 1981, I began my first journal and began to write as an out gay man. One of my poems, about a man I had a crush on, was mistaken for a Christian poem and was published in the Benedictine College English Department's journal. At the time I did not correct the misunderstanding in interpretation. I have taken on more challenges as a writer since making Atlanta my home six years ago. I am grateful for these opportunities, which have included *Cross Roads*, the newsletter for the African-American Lesbian Gay Alliance, and articles featured in *Etcetera Magazine* and *Southern Voice* (our proud les-bi-gay community weeklies)."

Ulysses: "I have witnessed Eurocentricity more destructive to brainwashed black men than racism, violence, drugs and alcohol combined. It haunts us so insidiously, I've developed an obsession that I write about. This is the first time I've published any of my artistic writings. I started writing last year when I sent someone a 'successful' anonymous love note — awakening my appreciation for both the artistry and power of words. Before then, I never read poems."

Vega was born in New York City on September 12, 1954. A graphic artist, poet and photographer, his work has appeared in the *Advocate*, *Blueboy*, *Black/Out*, *In The Life* and a self-published essay entitled *Men of Color* (1989). His company VEGA PRESS provides an outlet for other artists.

Richard Washington, Jr., was a writer involved with Other Countries. He studied voice at Julliard. He died in March 1991 of AIDS-related complications.

David Watts is a native New Yorker, who was educated at Yale and Harvard Universities. He currently works as a freelance editor and legal assistant. Beside issues of specifically gay and African-American concern, he is particularly interested in the study of languages, and in the eco-feminist response to such contemporary imaginative challenges as the irrevocable annihilation of living species, and the ever more pervasive coercions of the modern state. Born on February 7, 1950, he lives in New York City.

David Weems was born on November 21, 1961. He is a Baltimore-based photographer who is journeying into writing primarily through poetry based on his personal experiences. His photos have appeared in several publications, among them *Other Countries* and *The James White Review*. He is currently at work on a self-published collection of his photography and writing.

Robert Westley was born November 10, 1962. "I am a native of New Orleans where I spent my first seventeen years. I graduated from Northwestern University in 1984 with a B.A. in philosophy. I attended graduate school at Yale University for the following three years, and then started law school at the University of California, Berkeley, in f1987. I am currently working towards completion of my dissertation in philosophy and the final year of law school. My career plans include teaching, law practice, and economic development in the black community."

Marvin K. White was born on 4/29/66. He is being published for the first time in this anthology. Originally from Oakland, California, he now lives in Brooklyn, New York. He attends the City College of New York where he is majoring in theatre.

Michael Wiggins is a prominent member of ACT UP/NY. He has been arrested a number of times, including inside St. Patrick's Cathedral, for which he went on a celebrated trial.

Bob Williams was a forty-six-year old African-American short story writer and poet who lived in Washington, D.C. Bob was in the process of writing a collection of short stories on the lives of black gays at the time of his death in July 1991 due to AIDS-related complications.

John D. Williams lives and writes in East Orange, New Jersey.

Arthur T. Wilson—child of Elegua and Yemanja—poet, playwright and educator, received his graduate degrees at the New School for Social Research, New York University and the University of London. Recent plays include: *Naked Earth Songs, High Rise Snaps, For Those Who Have Grieved for Eleanor Bumpurs, Extended Family Sweet, Gretel Regrets, Life Sea Treasures,* and *Thunderbird Thorns Called Home.* Wilson's poetry appears in a number of literary journals and he is co-editor and founder of *Attitude Magazine,* President of Dance Giant Steps, Inc., and the director of Playwriting in the Schools at the New York Shakespeare Festival. He is currently working on two plays about AIDS-related issues for Health Watch's teenage repertory company funded by the Mayor's Office and the New York City Department of Health. Wilson is also the recipient of several artistic and civic awards and fellowships and is listed in *Who's Who in the East, Personalities of America* and other biographical references.

Phill Wilson is the founder of the Black Gay and Lesbian Leadership Forum, past co-chair of the Los Angeles chapter of Black and White

Men Together and one of the founders of the AIDS Hospice Foundation in Los Angeles. He is currently the AIDS coordinator for the City of Los Angeles.

Richard Witherspoon: Aframeric NY'er, loves to travel, he thinks... loving New York City as one who might have lived in Timbuktu, Carthage and Meroë. His work has appeared in *Spectrum, Lynx, The Red Pagoda, New Cicada, Other Countries, Black Men/White Men, Yemanja, Artist Pulp, 11th Assembling, Equal Time* and *Frogpond.* A collection of linked haiku is to appear in '93.

Donald Woods was born in December 1957. He has presented poetry as performance in many settings, including The Schomburg Library, P.S. 122, Art in the Anchorage and El Museo del Barrio in New York City; Painted Bride in Philadelphia; and Oval House in London. In print, his work has appeared in *Other Countries, In the Life, Brother to Brother* and other publications, including *The Space*: a ten-poem portfolio of his work published by Vexation Press in 1989.

Wrath is a poet, performance artist, and Philadelphian presently residing in Los Angeles. In 1989, a chapbook of his work entitled *The Horrors of Humanity* was released. His work has appeared in *Brother to Brother* and has been called "powerful and savage." A fellow poet has likened a reading by Wrath as tantamount to "being mugged by poetry."

Allen Wright, born on the Westside, raised on the Southside, lived on the Northside, only side left was east and that was the lake. Allen left Chicago for New York City where he fell in love with a man from Harlem. Allen now lives in Brooklyn. September 23rd is his birthdate.

Bil Wright: Poet, playwright, fiction writer. As a poet/playwright produced in N.Y.C.: La MaMa E.T.C., La MaMa La Galleria, BACA Downtown; represented the U.S. in The Best of New Dance/Theatre in Frankfurt, Germany, 1980; Yale University; Black Arts Festival in Atlanta, Georgia. Short fiction published in *Men on Men 3.* Currently at work on a novel.

Gary Paul Wright was born in Dallas, Texas, and has been a poet since the age of seven. In the years since then, he has been an actor, playwright, and director as well as a singer/songwriter. He is currently a New Yorker and active in the fight against AIDS.

INDEX OF TITLES

*Authors are listed alphabetically in the
Table of Contents.*

188

BOOKS AVAILABLE
FROM GALIENS PRESS

STATIONS, by Assoto Saint, $7.00. A cycle which traces the interracial love of two gay men as a celebration of survival, *Stations* stands as "a monumental testimony to the pain of experience and the beauty of love." The poems are stunning, painfully honest, richly crafted, and always full of surprises.

GALIENS PRESS
Box 4026
524 West 23rd Street
New York, NY 10011

Add $2.00 postage and handling for one book. For more than one book add an additional fifty cents per book. New York State residents please add appropriate sales tax. U.S. currency only. Personal checks or money orders please.

ABOUT THE EDITOR

Author of several theater pieces on the lives of gay black men, including *New Love Song,* **Assoto Saint** was born and raised in Haiti. His chapbook *Triple Trouble* was anthologized in *Tongues Untied* (GMP, London, 1987); his poetry collection, *Stations,* was published by Galiens Press in 1989. His writings have been anthologized in: *In the Life*; *New Men, New Minds*; *Gay & Lesbian Poetry in Our Time*; and *Brother to Brother.* They have appeared in: *Christopher Street, The Brooklyn Review, The James White Review, The PWA Coalition Newsline, Outweek, New York Native, Bay Windows, RFD, Other Countries, The Pyramid Periodical* and *Changing Men.* Saint was the poetry editor of the journal *Other Countries: Black Gay Voices.* He is also the lead singer of Xotika, an art-rock band, whose song "Forever Gay" is featured in the CD/cassette *Feeding the Flame,* released by Flying Fish Records, Inc. Saint was awarded a 1990 Fellowship in Poetry from the New York Foundation for the Arts. He was the recipient of the 1990 James Baldwin Award from the Black Gay & Lesbian Leadership Forum. His first play, *Risin' to the Love We Need* won second prize in the 1980 Jane Chambers Award for gay and lesbian playwriting. He is HIV-positive. He resides in New York City with his life-partner Jaan Urban Holmgren.